LESSONS FROM THE STORM

7 Steps to Turn Breakdowns into Breakthroughs

Melissa Myers

Copyright © 2025 Melissa Myers
BreakThruCrisis.com © 2025
All rights reserved

ISBNs
Paperback ISBN: 978-1-965761-29-8
eBook ISBN: 978-1-965761-30-4
Ingram Spark ISBN: 978-1-965761-31-1
Publisher: Spotlight Publishing House
https://spotlightpublishinghouse.com

Edited by Norma-Jean Strickland, Jade Vincent and Jamie McConochie
Book cover and design by Jamie McConochie

I'm not afraid of storms, for I am learning to sail my ship.

- Louisa May Alcott -

TABLE OF CONTENTS

ENDORSEMENTS … 7

ACKNOWLEDGEMENTS … 9

PROLOGUE – INTRODUCTION … 13

STEP 1 … 22
Solid Ground – Embodied Presence

STEP 2 … 32
My Allies – Support System

STEP 3 … 40
Awakened Heart – Develop Emotional Intelligence

STEP 4 … 52
Soul Anchor – Spiritual Connection

STEP 5 … 66
Mind Over Matter – Attitude

STEP 6 … 78
Training and Practice

STEP 7 … 84
Service – Share Your Wisdom

CONCLUSION … 90

ABOUT THE AUTHOR … 95

BIBLIOGRAPHY … 97

ENDORSEMENTS

As a Spiritual Teacher and Author, I am honored to celebrate my dear friend, Melissa Myers, for sharing her profound gift with those ready to break free from destructive cycles and step into the light their soul desires and deserves. If you're seeking a deeper understanding of how the Universe is working *for* you, not *to* you, I encourage you to read *Lessons from the Storm: 7 Steps to Turn Breakdowns into Breakthroughs*. Melissa's practical and transformative steps will guide you to turn your pain into a pathway back to love.
— **Sunny Dawn Johnston**, Author, Inspirational Speaker, Spiritual Teacher, and Psychic Medium

Through powerful personal storytelling of her own journey from breakdown to breakthrough, Melissa shares a profound pathway to inner freedom in her book *Lessons from the Storm*. The book combines poignant stories, intelligent references, poetic musings, and grounded activities to help the reader experience their own breakthrough through life's most challenging episodes.
— **Dr. Ashlee Greer**, Business Mindset Coach/Mentor, Trauma Expert, PhD in Counseling Psychology

As a longtime life coach and holistic wellness educator, I've always viewed breakdowns and breakthroughs as blessings! It's obvious Melissa Myers does too based on the inspirational and wise book she has written. Her compelling, easy-to-relate to steps will serve many on their path to healing and transformation. It's exciting to see one of our graduates excelling in her dream of touching lives and freeing souls.
— **KC Miller**, Founder Southwest Institute of Healing Arts — a conscious college community

Melissa's wisdom and heartfelt experience inspires the hope and tools needed to face our deepest feelings and tribulations from a place of courage, confidence and compassion. As a Coach and co-host for many years of one of the leading podcasts on Spotify based on emotional intelligence, I highly recommend Lessons from the Storm to anyone who longs for a deeper connection with themselves, others, and the unfolding of their precious life.
— **Monica Gonzalez**, CEO, Executive Coach & Mental Health Speaker

Melissa Myers has been both my client and a powerful success story. Once you read her book, you'll find yourself thinking, "Of course she is!" Melissa embodies everything she teaches, not as someone who learned from books alone, but as someone who leads from the heart and gut. She has journeyed through the deepest darkness, rediscovering how to ignite the light within—a light she once thought was lost forever.

Her 7 Lessons remind me of Dante's nine circles of hell, but with one key difference: Melissa offers a clear, actionable process for climbing out of your own personal "hell." Each of us carries some form of inner struggle, and while many blame themselves or others for their pain, Melissa teaches an empowering truth: you may not have caused the darkness, but healing it is your responsibility. No one can do it for you.

This book goes beyond theory. It's packed with meditations, practical coaching exercises, and no-nonsense guidance. It cuts through the fluff to deliver real, actionable wisdom. If you're on a self-development journey, this book isn't just a read—it's a tool, a companion, and a lifeline.

Easy to follow, fast to absorb, and overflowing with insights and practical tips, Melissa's work is an inspiration. I wholeheartedly recommend it to anyone seeking growth and transformation. Melissa, you are truly remarkable!
— **Marisa Ruiz**, Holistic Life Coach

As an actress and singer, I have always been in touch with my emotional body. As a dancer too, I have absolute control of my physical body. That's what happens on stage, not necessarily in my day-to-day life. When I realized that, I started to study coaching, meditation and yoga…

Lessons from the Storm, written by Melissa Myers, inspires deep change with simple, powerful tools. Of course this isn't an easy job, but she touches the part of you that you sometimes hide from yourself. If you work with this book, I promise, you will find treasures within. 🙏♡
— **Silvia Luchetti**, Actress, Singer, Vocal & Acting Coach

We all face pain, frustration, and rage along our path. We all have fears and, sooner or later, mildly, or profoundly, we all feel solitude. That's why this book is a must read for everyone looking to peacefully accept and learn from hardship instead of running, fighting, and hiding from it. The 7 steps Melissa presents in this book are truly helpful in part because they are so easy to follow. It takes this depth of personal experience, blended with raw honesty and generosity, to transform life's hardest lessons into something profoundly simple. Wherever there is a black hole, "Lessons from the Storm" is a beacon of light on top of the abyss, bringing clarity and hope to even the darkest of places. You just need to follow this light.
— **María Neila Martín**, Author, Professional Singer, NLP/Vocal coach.

This book provides you with a solid anchor in turbulent times.
— **Odile Van Hall**, M.D.

ACKNOWLEDGEMENTS

Of all the courses and training programs I've done, books and blogs I've read, videos I've watched, and places I've visited, I have ultimately learned the most from my relationships with others. Whether that be through momentary encounters that forever changed my perception or from deeper, long-standing friendships and partnerships throughout the years. It includes those who, for one reason or another, no longer form part of my life, but are forever part of my heart and soul.

Material wealth has not been easy for me to come by, partially because of negative beliefs carried in my subconscious or perhaps because wealth has never been a priority. I chose an unconventional path for my life and work. The way I have always felt rich is in the love that I have shared with my fellow human beings.

Despite all the pain I have experienced, traumas I have endured, and losses I have grieved, for the most part I have kept my heart open. This has allowed me the amazing gift of getting to know people from all walks of life, belief systems, mindsets, cultures, religions, sexual orientations, gender identifications, races, nationalities, and professions.

What I have discovered is that we are so much more alike than we are different. The surface aspects differ but, on the inside, we are far more the same. I've learned so much about my Self, about Life, about the Great Mystery... from each of you... family, friends, students, clients, teachers, mentors, therapists, coaches, partners, and lovers.

So, I want to thank you all from the very depths of my being. There is nothing I am more grateful for than you. It is because of you that I am still here, writing these words. This book is made possible because of you. Who I am has a huge part to do with you.

If your name doesn't appear on this list, it's not because you aren't important to my journey and to this book, because you are. If you are reading this, then you form a part of the constellation of my existence, and I honor you.

I like to say I have already lived at least three lives in this one. I started out in a little town in Upstate New York called Malone, then moved to Phoenix, Arizona and now live in the beautiful little pueblo in the Gredos Mountains of Spain, called Casavieja. In all those places and the ones visited in between, all throughout these 47 years, it would take far too many pages to name everyone who has touched my life and, in some way, contributed to this book. I'm going to name just some of the ones who are more directly involved in this book.

The first that comes to my heart is actually not a person, but my adorable, sweet, smart and cuddly companions and soul mates, Mirinda and Marley.

They have taught me more about unconditional love, commitment and putting love into practice than anyone.

I want to acknowledge in a huge way my life partner, Jamie McConochie, for more than I can say here. Without him, this book would not have been possible. His constant encouragement, as well as kind, warm, gentle, supportive, loving presence in my life has been truly a lifeline for me. It is because of him that you have such a stunningly beautiful book to read, as he spent weeks dedicating the majority of his days and countless hours in brainstorming and creating the work of art that this book has become. I cannot thank you enough, my love. This book is our book.

So many women have made this book possible that I cannot possibly name them all. The two who have contributed the most are my Mom, Jade Vincent, and my 106-year-old Grandma, Marjorie Myers. From these two powerful, resilient women, I have been given the greatest gifts a woman could ever hope for… immense love and generosity. They have taught me strength, hard work, spark and spunk, resourcefulness, determination and so much more. They have shown me, through their examples, what it means to learn from the storms and to turn breakdowns into breakthroughs.

To all of my "sis-stars," beautiful, bright, beams of light in my life, I am eternally grateful. Our circle reaches far, wide and deep into my heart, inspiring this book and my ability to break through and "let the light enter." We have listened, shared, learned, loved, lost, laughed, grieved, danced, grown, fallen and picked each other up. Without you, I would not have made it through many of the hard times, nor would I have had as much damn fun! Many of you have encouraged me to write this book for years and supported me all along the way as I have written it. Amy, Jenn, Misty, Irene, Mali, Kchi, Marina, Sara, Molly, Cori, Ana, Tere, Silvia, Carrie, Anna…

Amanda, God I miss you, pushing and punching me to wake up from my trances, loving, supporting and encouraging everything I ever did, never judging me. You, Mali and Kchi were my Fairy Godmothers; it's not the same without you. But you live on inside all of us and in this book. You would have loooooved it and been sooo excited for me! The first edition was released right around your birthday.

A special thanks to Sandy Rogers, for her role in my life as a sister, friend, second Mom and mentor, for helping edit, fund, publish and promote this book and for being another teacher of resilience, joy and fortitude. And to Becky Norwood for her generosity, professionalism and kindness. Sandy and Becky, thanks to you, this dream becomes a reality. To my Silver Sisters for the beautiful book we launched together and for motivating me to start writing again, I bow to you.

To all my teachers, mentors, therapists and coaches… Marisa, Dr. Ash, Ana, Dorian, Gabriel, Elena, Irene, Sunny, Samarah. Many of you held my hand and heart through the darkest nights of my soul and showed me over and over again the light of my own being. Others reflected back to me the infinite possibilities available to us. This book is a piece of all of you and all that we have accomplished together.

To my nieces and nephews, each of you have given and taught me more for this book and for my life than you will ever know. I have been awed and inspired by how you have already overcome so many obstacles in your young lives with such grace and power. Alina, Kira, Tristan, Josh, Fabian, Brooke, Kaylea... you are incredibly strong, resilient, kind, and bright lights in this world. I love you so much.

The circle would not be complete without mentioning the masculine pillar of my support system, those who go by the pronoun he... at least I think they all still do, ha-ha: Dave, David, Joselu, Glenn, Rudy, Adam, Oscar, Groovy T, D-rail, Mike... My Grandma always says I'm a lucky girl... Melissa and her boys, hahahha. She's right! I am a very lucky girl who has been blessed to share my life with men who have loved me deeply, provided the space for me to be able to blossom and spread my wings at my own pace, who offered a container of pure love without judgment, companionship, and mutual support whether that be through their role as partner, lover and/or friend. In spiritual visions, I have seen you standing around me, protecting, supporting, and holding space. Just your presence brings me peace and a feeling of safety.

And of course, my late fathers: Leigh Myers and Lee Vincent. I feel the two of you right there behind me in everything I do. Your love, your strength, and your memories are part of everything I do forever.

To all of my relations, loved ones and all my fellow human beings. Thank you for this shared gift of life. May we rise up together, through every storm, every dark night and help each other to break through our walls and discover the gold at the heart of it all. To all of those who are suffering, may we know deep and lasting peace.

Namaste and thank you!

PROLOGUE – INTRODUCTION

When going through a crisis of any kind, it often feels as though the ground beneath our feet begins to shake or even gives out. It feels like we are falling down a dark bottomless pit with nothing to hold onto. This can be extremely frightening. Oftentimes, we either become stuck and paralyzed or frantic and frenzied, which just plunges us into a deeper hole. We may come to the conclusion that our life is a complete mess, trapped in our ideas of how it/we should be. Some of us even get to the point where we feel like it's over, as if we don't have the strength to go on. This can be a crucial turning point, the point where we hit bottom and choose to rise.

Maybe your experience of crisis is less dramatic but equally debilitating. Do you get bogged down and hooked into your coping mechanisms and addictive behaviors to keep you distracted and numb from having to face whatever feels like too much? Have you found ways to keep it all under the surface, whilst deep down you know that an impending implosion is just around the corner?

This has been my own personal experience many times throughout my life. From losing loved ones, jobs, dreams, and relationships to facing feelings of inadequacy, deep fears, phobias, and traumas to dealing with conflicts with colleagues, family, friends, and partners. I, like you, and most other human beings, have had to deal with a variety of crises.

The good news is that I have come through each and every one. In the process, I have become quite skilled at handling them in a way that allows me to grow and evolve rather than fall apart. For that reason, I have created this 7-step process along with an in-depth online coaching program. My intention is to help you harness the lessons you've already learned, add some new ideas and skills, and awaken your inner guide. This will give you the strength, courage, and fortitude to face your current situation and any future ones.

If you are willing to commit to the inner work of training your mind, opening your heart, and anchoring into the wisdom of your soul, you will not only come through intact, but will be equipped to find the hidden gold. You will be able to take the opportunity offered from the crisis and turn your breakdowns into breakthroughs! You will become the hero/heroine of your own story, able to harness the power of the dragons and use it to serve yourself and the world.

That is what all successful, empowered, resilient people do and what this book is going to help you to do. This straightforward, easy to follow, and deeply transformative guide will help you to get through whatever difficult moment, problem, or crisis you are currently facing in a way that strengthens and expands who you are as a person. You will notice how your self-confidence and peace of mind increase, inspiring you to step up into a better version of yourself. Like the Phoenix, you will be able to rise from the ashes of whatever crisis you are facing or will face with renewed power and strength. You will

discover how it has propelled you to wake up, stand up, step up and fully rise and shine into a truer, fuller version of yourself.

In his book *Man's Search for Meaning*, first published in 1946, Austrian psychiatrist and survivor of the Holocaust, Victor Frankl said, "The last of the human freedoms is to choose one's attitude in any given set of circumstances" (Frankl, 2006).

You may not be able to change what's happening in your life that is causing you so much stress and anguish, but you absolutely can change the way you view it, the way you respond to it, your attitude about it...and that changes everything!

Some issues can and must be changed, others simply accepted and dealt with in the best way possible. Acceptance is not easy for us. We are more comfortable trying to exert control over life, but so much of this life is far beyond our control. In the steps outlined by Elisabeth Kübler-Ross for grieving (Kübler-Ross, 1969), *acceptance* is the final step where we are finally able to access some inner peace.

As the Serenity prayer reminds us:

> *"Grant me the Serenity to accept the things I cannot change, the Courage to change the things I can and the Wisdom to know the difference."*

I'd like to share a personal story as an example. Some years ago, I went through a major crisis in my relationship with my partner as well as within myself. The traumatic experiences from my childhood and teen years had left me with many deep scars, including one that showed up in the form of toxic jealousy. I had been that way as long as I could remember. In my first serious relationships, I had always justified it. In other words, if I felt jealous, it must be because my partner was doing something wrong. At least that's what I had convinced myself. In painful arguments and fights, I would vehemently try to convince my significant other that he was the one who shouldn't have been talking to another woman...period. However, I had begun to realize just how unfair and toxic my attitude was for my partner and for myself. I desperately wanted to change it.

Change is a process, just as becoming a certain way or getting to a specific breaking point is something that has built up over time. Undoing, unlearning, and breaking through are also evolutions. Breakdowns and breakthroughs may sound and feel like something that just happened suddenly but, in reality, they are a gradual progression that eventually come to a culmination.

This was the case with my jealousy. My first experiences with relationships were anything but healthy. In fact, they were traumatic, which left its imprint on me, as it does on all of us. One of the symptoms showed up in my life in the

> *The last of the human freedoms is to choose one's attitude in any given set of circumstances.*
>
> - Victor Frankl

form of extreme jealousy and the need to control my partner. This had caused problems in all my relationships throughout my life, and it finally came to a head with my husband at the time. We would argue; I would get really worked up trying to justify my feelings and, in the process, make him feel responsible for them. We would go round and round in this very destructive, debilitating, and damaging cycle.

My awareness of what was happening inside of me was different this time. I had been regularly practicing meditation and Mindfulness, studying Transpersonal Psychology, and doing therapy for the first time in my life. This had opened a whole new perspective and understanding. It had also given me some tools and the training that was beginning to help me respond instead of react. I was learning how to be with what was coming up inside of me, to acknowledge the "visitors" as Rumi describes them in his poem, *Guest House*.

> This being human is a guest house.
> Every morning a new arrival.
>
> A joy, a depression, a meanness,
> some momentary awareness comes
> as an unexpected visitor.
>
> Welcome and entertain them all!
> Even if they're a crowd of sorrows,
> who violently sweep your house
> empty of its furniture,
> still, treat each guest honorably.
> He may be clearing you out
> for some new delight.
>
> The dark thought, the shame, the malice,
> meet them at the door laughing,
> and invite them in.
>
> Be grateful for whoever comes,
> because each has been sent
> as a guide from beyond.

"Guest House" by RUMI

Most people lack emotional intelligence. We don't know ourselves very well and don't understand our emotions. We tend to do the opposite of what Rumi invites us to do in his poem. Instead of inviting feelings in and learning how to be with them, we slam the door and run in the opposite direction as fast as we can. Maybe we catch a glimpse of some inner wounded part of ourselves, but then we lock her in the basement and throw away the key, hoping she will never come back and bother us again.

We use a wide variety of strategies to keep our wounded inner child at bay. In doing so, we condemn ourselves to a half-lived existence where much of our vital life force energy is wasted running and hiding from ourselves. It's a continuous, tremendously challenging, and empowering process to develop the capacity to welcome and attend to all of our feelings and emotions.

I was one of those people trying to skip over the deep emotional wounds from my childhood that showed up in all kinds of creative and distorted ways throughout the years. If you lock a child in the basement for over 20 years, how do you expect her to communicate and perceive reality? The Internal Family Systems Psychotherapy method explains how our exiled inner parts wreak havoc on our lives in their desperate attempts to get our attention, protect us and get our/their needs met. Many of us were emotionally abandoned as children and we then continue the cycle in adulthood, abandoning ourselves day after day in a myriad of different ways.

I was skidding down a very rough road that seemed to get worse before it got better. At one point, both my husband and I were starting to get worried that I was really "losing it." I had begun to argue out loud with those "visitors," not only with him, but with the voices in my mind. Perhaps that makes me sound like an insane person, "the voices in my head." But if we pay attention, we realize that we all have them and often engage in full on narratives that completely, and usually quite unconsciously, control our lives.

At the Transpersonal Psychology school, I learned about some of these "Visitors," "Inner Voices" or "Parts." An example is the "Wounded Inner Child" who is trapped in some dungeon within us and continues to experience life from that small, hurt, scared, vulnerable little one who didn't get their innermost needs met in their childhood. I also learned about, experienced, and was developing, "The Witness." This is the part of our Inner Self who is able to observe, from a more neutral perspective, whatever is happening without getting caught up in it. During that tumultuous time, I also discovered within myself other "visitors" that I named "The Instigator" (or Lawyer), and "The Judge."

The Instigator would egg me on whenever the jealousy got triggered, telling me that I was right, my partner was wrong and that I had every right to be angry because it was really his fault. The Judge would then turn on me and tell me that I was bad, a terrible person who was hurting the people she loved and that I was to blame, it was really all my fault. So, I started to bounce around from the wounded Inner Child reacting, in fits of rage and tears, to the Instigator fueling the fire, to the Judge making me feel like a complete piece of shit for how I was behaving.

I eventually began to practice taking myself out of the situation and going to sit in meditation to try to manage the intense waves of emotions and fast, frantic thoughts, while connecting to and taking refuge in the Inner Witness.

It was a messy, scary, clumsy process and after a while both my partner and I were quite worn out from it all. But there was hope, something was changing, even though it was slow and complex. I didn't give up. I kept practicing what I was learning, even when it seemed impossible and like I would never be able to get rid of it. I soon came to realize that the desperate attempt to try to "get rid of it" was precisely what maintained its tight grip on me.

Finally, that breakthrough moment came. In this case, it was one specific moment from which everything completely changed. A burst of deep insight, freedom and surrender came that forever altered my experience of relationships and of my inner journey.

I remember it very clearly although it was many years ago. My partner was packing and preparing his trip to India, a voyage he would embark on within a few days that intensely triggered all my fears and jealousy. I had encouraged him to go because I knew how important it was to him. However, that meant I had to endure continual, intense inner dialogue that turned into arguments with him about how threatening it was to our relationship. He would surely meet lots of interesting, attractive women during the month-long journey, and I wouldn't be there to stop it from happening.

I was washing the dishes when the Inner Instigator realized that my husband would miss my birthday, and my Inner Child began feeling abandoned and hurt. He realized something was wrong and began to ask me. This was that crucial point where the argument usually started. The Inner Lawyer would make their case, laying out all the reasons why my pain and jealousy were justified. This would result in my husband feeling as though it was his fault.

But this time I did something totally different. In fact, I did the exact opposite of what I had been doing. Instead of fighting with myself, with him and with reality, I surrendered. I took a deep breath and said, *"You want to know what's wrong? I am feeling triggered. You are leaving soon, and I'm scared. It's not your fault and it's not mine, but this is coming up again. It feels intense and I'm just trying to deal with it."*

Whew! It was a like a huge weight was lifted from my shoulders and from his. There was no blame, no reason to argue or fight, nothing to prove or protect. There was just vulnerability, honesty and sincerity which opened the space for love. He gave me a gentle, kind, forgiving hug and we both relaxed and opened. It was a huge breakthrough in a process that had involved years of breakdowns and turmoil.

It's not to say I have never felt jealous since; of course I have. But the jealousy no longer holds power over me. I am now able to welcome it when it comes to visit. I can offer refuge and some kindness to this small, scared part of me, while knowing that it doesn't define who I am. I am not the jealousy. I am more like the host to this weary visitor traveling its way along my psyche. I am not the little girl who was abused and abandoned. I am a conscious woman, able to take care of her inner world.

Maybe you are currently facing something similar and in need of some peace of mind and clarity. My hope is that this book can serve as a kind of lifeline to your inner strength, creativity, and wisdom. That it will help you, not only get through difficult times, but to come out of them more alive and empowered than before. Every breakdown has the potential to become a breakthrough.

There is no doubt that life can certainly be very hard. If you are reading this, I imagine you are going through something challenging. I assure you, you can and will get through it.

My father used to always tell me that "bad things happen in threes." There is that expression, "When it rains, it pours" referring to the often-strange phenomena that when things start to go awry in our lives, one thing leads to another, and it starts to seem like we have a black cloud over our head dampening every area of our lives. We deal with one problem and another sprouts up right after. This can start to weigh heavy on us, and we can end up feeling worn down, like we just can't take it anymore. We start to tell ourselves, "There must be something wrong with me," or "I'm just unlucky," or "Everything always happens to me," "I can't deal with this," "I don't know what to do," and so on. Then it becomes a self-fulfilling prophecy because our brains believe what we tell them.

We often get so blocked that we genuinely don't know what to do or where to go from here. We go round and round in circles in our mind, but we don't take the actual steps that bring us any relief or generate real solutions. Partially that is because, as Einstein said, "No problem can be solved from the same level of consciousness that it was created."

I know what it's like, which is why I've created this method of 7 steps. Using both modern and ancient findings from Neuroscience, Mindfulness, Transpersonal Psychology, and Somatics, we are going to re-program your limiting ideas, thoughts, and beliefs. At the same time, you will re-connect to your inner reservoir of strength and resilience so that you know that you can, will be and are more than capable of facing this and whatever comes your way. Get ready to blow off that pesky black cloud and rise into your power!

This book outlines a step-by-step process to turn breakdowns into breakthroughs. We will be working with the physical, mental, emotional, and spiritual aspects of your being. This is a holistic approach to managing your life. All of these aspects of our being influence our experience of situations and, therefore, must be addressed for deep and lasting transformation to occur. As you enhance your Emotional Intelligence, Resilience, and Intuition, you will appreciate a revitalized and more empowered perspective. This helps you develop the capacity to experience whatever happens without falling apart, but rather rising up with hope, confidence and trust.

My life so far has been a "long strange trip," as *The Doors* put it, or we could say a kind of epic journey, filled with plenty of breakdowns and breakthroughs. My childhood was full of wonderful moments, yet pointedly marked by tragedy and trauma. As a young child and teen, I experienced sexual abuse, domestic violence, bullying, loss of close loved ones through death and divorce, just to name some of the intense life experiences that contributed to my breakdowns. I won't go into all the details here but will continue to share a few personal stories throughout this book about how I have been able to use the crises in my own life as opportunities and how you can, too!

I have gratitude for everything I've been through, including the darkest most difficult stuff, as it all forms part of what has made me who I am today. My coach asked me to name five positive things that came from all my trauma, which provoked the deep realization that who I am, everyone who is in my life, all that has happened so far is intertwined with the past hardships. I am finally beginning to truly love myself and, therefore, I don't want to be someone different. I want to keep becoming more fully who I am. And who I am is made up of a mixture of my Essence or Soul, as well as my personality formed partially from the qualities I developed through crises.

A hero/heroine doesn't become that way by coasting through life with no challenges. They have to face dragons, danger and death repeatedly. It is by facing their fears and demons that they are able to step into their power. There are lots of things I am still working through and probably always will. This continues to provide me with important opportunities, "grist for the mill," as they say. It really boils down to how we look at challenges and what we choose to do with them when they inevitably come up again and again. They could keep us trapped in The Victim or give us all the tools to be a hero/heroine.

My early experiences were traumatic and often it is those traumas that later cause us to "break down" as we get older. Or perhaps our childhood was fairly healthy but later in life we faced situations that were so painful we began to lose or close ourselves off. Either way, when we come to our breaking point, it is those breakdowns that offer us a portal, a doorway, that perhaps others cannot see. If we have the courage to open and walk through, we are granted access to powerful aspects of our being: depth, wisdom, strength, and capacities that otherwise we may never have encountered.

So, let's get down to the nitty gritty. How do we turn breakdowns into breakthroughs?

Here are 7 Steps that will help you to do just that.

Mindfulness teacher Shauna Shapiro (2009) says, "What we practice grows stronger." These steps will not work for you if you only read about them. They are steps that must be taken, day after day, moment by moment, over and over again. If you do that persistently, consistently, I promise you will see results. I strongly encourage you to commit to this, go at your own pace, find your rhythm, and honor this process and everything in life.

One way to do this could be to focus on one step per week, not necessarily in chronological order. Read through the steps and allow yourself to feel which one would be most helpful for you to start with. Bear in mind that sometimes the one that is the most intimidating is actually the one we most need.

> *Out of suffering have emerged the strongest souls; the most massive characters are seared with scars.*
>
> — Khalil Gibran

"The Great Belly of Existence"

Even in the darkest hours, there are infinite points of light.

Sometimes like glints of hope they come through the kind words of a friend,

Or the sound of the birds singing outside the window.

Even when the shades are pulled all the way down,

and darkness fills the room,

Sometimes just their persistent melody guides us toward the light.

Those long, dark nights when our fears grip us in the blackness,

A single ray of moonlight pierces its way through and reminds us we are not alone.

And when no light appears from outside

and the world itself seems to have been swallowed whole,

If we allow ourselves to be digested and integrated into

the Great Belly of Existence,

Perhaps we discover that the Universe with its eternal darkness and infinite light, reaching across all the dimensions of time and space,

forms of life and death,

has always been within us, every step of the way.

Every laugh, every tear,

Every triumph, every fear.

Intrinsically, inevitably, and undeniably intertwined.

~ Melissa Myers, 2018 ~

STEP 1:

SOLID GROUND - EMBODIED PRESENCE

*"Deep in their roots,
all flowers keep the light."*

-Theodore Roethke-

STEP 1:
SOLID GROUND – EMBODIED PRESENCE

Embodied presence is our ability to be with what's happening without dissociating, repressing, or avoiding it. Instead, we learn to hold space, keep calm, resource, and regulate the nervous system. We come out of the looping narrative in the mind and drop down into the body.

When something difficult is happening in our lives, our tendency is to desperately try to control it and/or avoid it. There is nothing inherently wrong with these strategies. They have helped us to survive and have their place. However, the frantic, desperate, unconscious way we often *react*, blocks us from being able to effectively *respond*.

When we experience hardships or trauma, our limbic system, aka survival brain, can become over-active and be in a hypervigilant state, trying to exert some kind of control over what is happening or make sure that those bad things don't happen again (hyper-arousal). Or we may shut down and become stuck in lethargy and procrastination (hypo-arousal), in an effort to numb ourselves and avoid more disappointment and pain.

Yet so much of life simply cannot be controlled. It is uncertain, wild, ever-changing, delicate and exquisitely unpredictable. If we want to live a full, authentic life, we must come to terms with the unknown. The alternative is to merely exist, in gray scale mode at best. I don't know about you, but I'm far too fond of colors for that.

Let's explore more about our Brain, Nervous System, Survival Response and how they impact our experience of the challenges we face.

Our nervous system controls most of what we think, how we feel and what our body does.

> A healthy (autonomic) nervous system ebbs and flows from the sympathetic (which is responsible for action and survival) to the parasympathetic (whose function governs "rest and digest"). A nervous system in crisis or on the verge of a breakdown is more often stuck in hyper-arousal (foot stuck on the gas) or hypo-arousal (foot stuck on the brake).

The limbic system is the survival part of our brain and habitually obsesses over the past and the future with the intention to protect us by showing us what went wrong and what could go wrong.

This hyper-vigilance causes anxiety, tension, stress and all the illnesses that go along with it.

We may get good at surviving, but life is so much more than that.

Learning to regulate our nervous system helps us feel calmer, safer and more capable of handling what is happening. Therefore, we are able to face our situation in a more effective way, without the desperation.

This begins with learning to come into our body and out of our looping, fearful, frantic thoughts. It means going from the dissociated "safe place" we sometimes zone out to, and coming back to the present moment, even if it is challenging.

It means we stop running, fighting, and hiding long enough to truly see what is in front of us. We finally turn to face the "tiger" or "dragon" or whatever feels threatening. We can do this because we are sourced from an empowered place within that begins with a deep connection to our bodies.

For many years, I was stuck in this Survival Response. Looking back, it's hard to say exactly how or when it happened. Like so many of us, I was rather used to my coping mechanisms and survival responses, as were those around me. They kind of morphed into part of my personality.

I was hyper-active, fiery, ambitious, and overly social. I hated being alone. In fact, I was terrified of it. I couldn't stop for long and had to constantly being doing something. (That's still hard for me, I must admit, but nowhere near how it used to be.) I filled my schedule as full as possible. My moments, days, weeks and life in general were as crammed full as could be. I had my significant other, family, friends, work, projects, studies to occupy my time and energy. As long as I kept myself busy, all was "well," at least on the surface.

But deep down I knew that all was not well. I was terrified of being alone because I was terrified of the skeletons buried within the closets of my psyche.

There is a powerful quote I read many years ago that struck a chord deep within me. I'm not sure if it came from the Gospel of Thomas or the Dead Sea Scrolls or where, but its message is clear:

"If you bring forth what is within you, what you bring forth will save you. If you do not bring forth what is within you, what you do not bring forth will destroy you."

It took me many years and much suffering before I mustered up the courage to begin to summon those skeletons. But once I did, there was no stopping.

When I left the U.S. on the adventure that eventually led me to my home in Spain, I threw away my agenda, all my plans, my phone and everything that had kept me in my comfort zone with its illusion of safety or as my Coach, Marisa Ruiz calls it, my "Comfort Cell." I took a brave leap into the unknown with the intention of bringing forth what was within me, no matter how frightened of it I was. I was tired of living in that bubble, skirting around the fear, trying to stay one step ahead of it.

All along the way, I was continuously confronted with *all that was within me*, which consisted of a whole lot of fear and a big dose of shame to go along with it. I would ultimately discover an immense well of strength, wisdom and love right on the other side of that fear and shame. But, first, I would get trapped for many years in a long, dark tunnel that I didn't know if I would ever escape.

That tunnel was largely comprised of my Survival Response *stuck* in overdrive.

It was strongly triggered by not being able to speak the language. When people would speak to me and I couldn't understand them, my heart would pound so hard I thought it would explode out of my chest. A feeling of profound discomfort would flood through my whole body whenever I tried to string together a sentence with the few words I had learned in Spanish and people either chuckled or stared back at me with a look that said they had no idea what I was trying to say.

This ongoing experience over the course of many years as I struggled to learn Spanish, combined with the culture shock, in an environment so different than the one I was used to, was more than my nervous system could bear.

What began to happen was that every time I would go out to a store, restaurant or run into someone on the street, the survival response would kick in. My heart would start pounding, adrenaline would flood my system and, as a result, my face would turn bright red. People would sometimes point out and comment on it which would mortify me even more, causing my face to flush a deeper, brighter shade of red. And so it went that I began to anticipate these encounters and dread them.

The only real stability I had in my life at the time was my relationship with my husband. When that ended in 2012, it sent me over the edge of the narrow tightrope I had been trying to walk on.

My sympathetic nervous system spiked into overdrive, bouncing from fight to flight to freeze to fawn as an almost perpetual state of being.

Even though my Spanish had dramatically improved, my blushing saga intensified, and I began to avoid encounters with people as much as possible, except for situations where I could have a few drinks, which would help calm that survival response. My erythrophobia (fear of blushing) turned into full blown social anxiety and agoraphobia.

I went from being terrified of being alone, to having a phobia of most social situations. Walking into a store or sitting at a table to have a meal with other people felt like life threatening situations. To make matters worse, I felt deeply ashamed of myself for feeling the way I did. When I tried to explain it to people, no one understood, and I felt more and more isolated.

All the while, I was studying Transpersonal Psychology and receiving therapy. In 2016, I was diagnosed with Complex Post Traumatic Stress Disorder, but I basically discarded the diagnosis until many years later when I began to work with a Somatic Trauma Informed Coach. Through the skillful and loving guidance of my Coach, I was able to begin to reinhabit my body and very slowly reacquaint myself with the exiled parts of my psyche – such as the shame and fear I had been running from all my life.

Somatic Work is a crucial first step when we are going through a crisis. It helps us to establish a felt sense of safety and resource the fight/flight/freeze/fawn response when it gets triggered.

A Tibetan monk once told me, "Surrender to the tiger, and you will see that it is just a little kitty cat."

This is the power of somatics, of embodiment work. Somatics invites us to form a FELT relationship with ourselves and our own wisdom by sensing our experience from the inside.

I first learned the term "grounding" when I did my yoga teacher training. It is an apt description of the process we are going to learn together now. As I mentioned earlier, when we are going through a crisis, it can feel as if the ground beneath our feet is giving way. We may feel like our whole world and very existence is shaking and in danger. We must learn to find solid ground, especially in the midst of the storm.

That solid ground is within us. One way we can access it is by connecting to the actual ground we are standing on and coming back into our body.

When we are scared or upset, our mind and heart start racing. From this fight-or-flight response in our nervous system, we may be able to outrun or fight off a tiger or other predator (as was the original purpose of this response). However, we won't be able to access the more evolved, creative parts of our brain (the pre-frontal cortex). We need that part to effectively cope with our situation, which most likely is not truly life-threatening, even though it may feel that way.

Even if it is a life-threatening situation, such as a terminal illness, we will be much more capable of going through it in the best way possible if we access these more developed parts of our brain. The parts where resilience, courage, compassion, and creativity abide. Freaking out or shutting down only agitates, escalates, and aggravates whatever we are experiencing. We are learning how to keep calm and navigate through the storm.

COPING WITH CRISIS TOOLKIT

Somatic practices are some of the best ways to regulate the nervous system and restore a felt sense of safety to our entire being. Memories are stored in the body. Tension in the body feeds fear and anxiety and vice versa. It is crucial to release stored trauma, as well as presently held emotional turbulence from our bodies on a regular basis. It is a game changer on all levels.

"When we're unable to feel, we cannot integrate. Without integration, we miss out on the chance and inherent right to engage fully in life." Maanee Chrystal, the Somatic Institute for Women.

There are many things that can help us be more present in our bodies (and lives) such as exercise, sports, yoga, martial arts, walking, dancing, singing, jumping, going barefoot, and so on.

I want to share with you my "Coping with Crisis Toolkit" which has three techniques to help you "ground yourself" and embody safety in moments of crisis:

1

Practice 1: Soft Belly

This is a very simple technique developed by an expert in trauma and resilience, James Gordon, M.D. (2019). He has it used with thousands of trauma survivors to help them turn their crisis experience from debilitating to moving through the stages to managing the after-effects and then finally feeling alive and empowered. Sit in a comfortable position with your back straight and feet on the floor. Relax your body as much as possible and begin taking deep breaths while at the same time repeating the mantra "Soft Belly."

On the inhale, out loud or in your mind, you say, "soft" and on the exhale "belly."

Do this for as long as you feel like and notice the changes in your body and mind.

Practice 2

Stand with your back straight, shoulders down and relaxed and feet hip-width apart. Close your eyes or you can keep them slightly open looking down toward the ground. Try to relax your body, especially belly, hands, arms, shoulders, and neck which tend to tense up. Connect with your breath, inhaling and exhaling slowly, deeply, and consciously. Really pay attention to and feel each breath as it comes in and out. Fill up the belly with air on the in-breath and let go of the breath and tension in the body and mind on the out-breath. If thoughts come into your mind, allow them to just float by, imagining them like clouds in the sky while you just bring your attention back again and again to the breath, re-relaxing the body as many times as necessary.

Now put all your attention into the soles of your feet. Feel any sensations there such as tingling, throbbing, heat or cold. Feel them in contact with the solid ground beneath them and the Earth below that. If you are able to do this outdoors barefoot, even better. If not, you can imagine the Earth beneath your feet, grass, sand, or rock, and allow the feeling to bring you a sense of calm and strength. Now, you can imagine roots extending from the soles of your feet down, down, down, deep into the Earth almost as though you are a great, strong tree, perhaps an Oak or a Maple Tree.

Feel your connection to the Earth and her energy, strength, calm and confidence spiraling up through those roots into your feet, filling your entire body, mind, and heart. Stay this way, feeling the feet on the ground, body relaxed and deep breathing as long as you feel is necessary until you feel grounded, centered and ready to continue forward.

Practice 3

Trauma experts and researchers have proven that shaking and trembling are extremely effective methods of restoring our body back to its natural, efficient state during and/or after experiencing crisis. This prevents it from becoming a trauma and releases stored negative memories in the body and mind.

This practice is based on the work of Dr. Peter Levine who developed the concept of "somatic experiencing." Levine observed that wild prey animals, though threatened routinely, are rarely traumatized. When an animal experiences a life-threatening shock, it will go into a state of extreme shaking and trembling as the shock is processed and passed through its body.

> "Animals in the wild utilize innate mechanisms to regulate and discharge the high levels of energy arousal associated with defensive survival behaviors. These mechanisms provide animals with a built-in 'immunity' to trauma that enables them to return to normal in the aftermath of highly 'charged' life-threatening experiences." (Levine, n.d.)

In humans, the rational part of our brains often inhibits our ability to effectively regulate the impact of traumatic experiences the way animals do. Consequently, our nervous system stays out of balance because we don't properly release the survival energies, so they get stuck in our bodies. The symptoms that we experience from trauma come from our attempts to manage and contain this unused energy. Levine asserts that the way for humans to dispel traumatic symptoms is to physically shake it off, just as wild animals do.

If the stress, tension, and anxiety you are experiencing is especially intense, it is very helpful to jump, shake and move our bodies. There are many ways to do this such as putting on some music and just dancing, moving however we feel like. Jumping up and down while making sounds such as "Huh" or "Ah" helps us to let go and come into our body. We can also just shake our body back and forth, up and down and all around as we imagine the tension and stress kind of dissipating and shaking out of us.

When you finish, just sit down, rest and allow the experience to integrate into your body and psyche. You will find that you feel more relaxed, less anxious, and lighter.

YOUR BREAKTHROUGH PLAN FOR STEP 1

1. Pay special attention to your body this week, noticing the tendency to tense up, hold your breath, rush around or dissociate. When you notice any of these reactions, just gently relax back into the present moment, feeling your feet on the ground, deepening the breath and slowing down. Perhaps come up with a mantra to help you remember. To give you some ideas, here are examples I often use:

   - "My essence is at ease"
   - "I am safe"
   - "It's okay, I've got this"

   Connect with stillness.

2. Do one of these techniques every day, and every time you start to feel overwhelmed, scared, or stuck.

3. Spend as much time in nature as you can and/or practicing yoga, dance, martial arts, sports or other physical activities. Move your body, move the energy, release the fear and other stuck emotions.

STEP 2:

MY ALLIES – SUPPORT SYSTEM

*"How did the rose ever open its heart and
give to this world all of its beauty?
It felt the encouragement
of light against its being.
Otherwise, we all remain too scared."*

~Hafez~

STEP 2:
MY ALLIES – SUPPORT SYSTEM

When we encounter life's storms, it's easy to feel isolated and overwhelmed. However, it is precisely during these times that we need to lean into the dual pillars of inner strength and external support. Cultivating both inner resources and outer connections allows us to navigate hardships with greater resilience and grace.

Developing inner resources means taking the time to fortify your emotional, mental, and spiritual reserves. This involves practices such as mindfulness, meditation, journaling, and self-reflection. These tools help us reconnect with our inner voice, reminding us that we have survived challenges before and possess the strength to overcome them again. Inner resources also include cultivating a mindset of self-compassion, where we treat ourselves with the kindness and understanding we'd offer a cherished friend.

At the same time, life's challenges remind us that we are not meant to endure struggles alone. Building and leaning on outer connections is not a sign of weakness but of wisdom. Reaching out to friends, family, and trusted confidants creates a safety net of care and encouragement. Professional support, such as from therapists or counselors, provides guidance and a fresh perspective that can be invaluable during tough times.

There is profound strength in vulnerability. Allowing others to see us in our moments of difficulty fosters deeper, more meaningful relationships. By sharing our struggles, we invite empathy, understanding, and solidarity—and often find that others are eager to extend their support.

When going through hard times, it is essential to connect to your inner strength and resilience. Use your current tool belt and add whatever new tools are needed. Also remember to reach out and allow yourself to receive support from friends, family, therapists, counselors, and others. We need to support ourselves in the best possible way, to show up for ourselves, as we would with a dear friend who is going through a hard time. It's time to bring forth all the love we can muster and surround ourselves with it.

My "Regroup & Reconnect Reflection" is a great practice to take stock of the support systems you have available in your life, and to develop those further.

1

Practice 1: Taking Stock

Current Tool Belt

Make a list of the resources you already have within and around you:

1. Do you have some notches under your belt on a personal growth or spiritual journey that you can refer to for guidance?
2. Maybe you took some classes or read some books about mindfulness or meditation that you can start to apply to your current situation.
3. What about the breathing techniques from yoga or Pilates classes?
4. Use the tools you currently have, the things you have learned so far, as well as the innate inner qualities that you have further developed along the way.
5. What are your strengths?
6. What are you good at?
7. How would someone who knows you well and loves you describe you?
8. What are your best qualities?
9. If you were ready to face the battle that would save the world and earn you your rightful place in it, what dormant capacities would you need to call upon?
10. How can you put them to use now to face whatever is currently happening in your life?

New Tools Needed

Observe with neutrality and non-judgment:

1. What are your weaknesses?
2. What are you lacking that could help you now?
3. What skills, abilities, or characteristics need further development to move through this effectively?
4. When and how are you going to do that?
5. Reading this book is a good start, so give yourself a pat on the back for that!

When Hercules set out to slay the Hydra, first he had to either acquire, create, or at least sharpen his sword.

What elements do you need to acquire, create, or sharpen in order to continue your quest?

Current Network

Who are the people in your life that you can truly count on? Consider those who genuinely know how to show up, hold space, and stand by your side as you confront the shadows and uncertainties of your life. These are the individuals who offer unwavering presence without judgment, and whose support feels like a steady anchor in turbulent times.

On the other hand, reflect on relationships that may unintentionally keep you tethered to old patterns. Are there people in your life who, while well-meaning, encourage you to stay in your comfort zone? Do their actions—or inactions—subtly discourage growth by avoiding the deeper work of awareness and accountability? As Dr. Gabor Maté discusses in his book *In the Realm of Hungry Ghosts* (2010), such dynamics can inadvertently feed our "hungry ghosts"—those coping mechanisms or habits that no longer serve us but feel difficult to release.

> *True connection and intimacy are developed through vulnerability.*

This is not about judging or trying to change others but about prioritizing self-care. It's a matter of recognizing how we invest our most precious resources: our time and energy. Thoughtful boundaries empower us to nurture healthier relationships with both ourselves and those around us. As Jessica Moore wisely states, "Our boundaries define our personal space – and we need to be sovereign there in order to step into our full power and potential."

During times of difficulty, we may feel more vulnerable and susceptible to external influences. Being mindful of the company we keep is essential. There are people we love deeply, yet we might need to limit our interactions with them, especially when our own reserves are low. By doing so, we protect our well-being while still maintaining the essence of those relationships.

We inevitably influence and are influenced by those around us. It's worth considering: Are the people in your circle helping you to rise to your best self, or are they inadvertently contributing to stagnation? When you have friends or connections that uplift and inspire you, take a moment to recognize and celebrate that. Gratitude for these relationships reinforces their positive impact on your life.

Now, ask yourself: Do you truly count on them, allow them in, lean on them when you are struggling? Or do you try to do it all on your own, hide your fears and tears behind a smiley face mask?

Many of us learned to have a stiff upper lip and just kind of suck it up and get on with it. After talking with some of my clients and loved ones facing terminal illness, many of them revealed that much of their suffering came from the feeling that they were falling short and being a burden, simply by having gotten sick, as if they were somehow to blame.

Do you know that true connection and intimacy are developed through vulnerability? To feel close to each other, we have to be willing to reveal our trembling hearts, messy minds and our imperfect, bumbling humanness.

We aren't doing ourselves or anyone else any favors when we hide our trials and tribulations and try to put on a show about how fine we are. Social media can be a breeding ground for this kind of superficial performance-type relating that ends up alienating and isolating humans from other humans. Nobody's life is perfect nor is it a competition, even when it seems to be portrayed as such.

Unfortunately, much of society's conditioning would have us think that perfection exists. Quite often we feel we are failing somehow, losing at the game of life, especially compared to our colleagues' posts on Facebook. This happens even more so when times are tough in our own lives.

Years ago, I read a profoundly inspiring book called, *Broken Open: How Difficult Times Can Help Us Grow,* by Elizabeth Lesser. I highly recommend it for anyone going through crisis. It is filled with wisdom, encouragement and deeply moving stories about people just like you and me, blundering through this thing called life, doing the best we can. It demonstrates how those of us who feel called, sometimes even shoved, can learn to dive a little deeper below the surface of our struggles and rise up stronger like the Phoenix.

She has a chapter in the book called *Bozos on the Bus,* which is perhaps one of my favorites. The idea comes from a clown-activist during the 1970s called Wavy Gravy. Elizabeth says:

> "…we are all bozos on the bus, contrary to the self-assured image we work so hard to present to each other on a daily basis. We are all half-baked experiments -- mistake-prone beings, born without an instruction book into a complex world." (Lesser, 2004)

Our support system is largely comprised of the people in our lives and how we relate to each other. When going through hardships, it can make all the difference to reach out and feel our connection, our belonging. It can help us remember how we are all "bozos on the bus" as well as potential hero/heroines, and that the two are not exclusive of one another.

Connectify Plan

1. How can you meet more of the kind of people who can enrich your life?
2. Are there any support groups where you live or online that could be useful during this challenging time?
3. How about a class, meet-up group or event where you could begin to connect with others?

Practice 2: Belonging Meditation

Close your eyes, turn your gaze inward, and connect with your breath. Use your awareness to come fully into the present moment. Feel your body sitting or lying on the chair or ground. Use this sacred pause to just relax your muscles, steady your breathing and slow your brain activity and heart rate.

Take a few minutes to just allow yourself to settle into this guided meditation.

Begin by feeling the contact of your body with the ground and earth beneath you. feel your connection to the earth, how she holds you up and supports you. As you breathe, become aware of how the very air that is flowing into and out of your body is made of the oxygen released by her plants and trees. It's the same air that is recycled and shared by all the other living beings on this beautiful planet. Give thanks for how her many fruits nourish and sustain you. Take a moment to bask in the awe and wonder of forming part of the great web of life. Touch the ground beneath or beside you, as Buddha did under the Bodhi tree, and remember that you are a strand that forms part of the web. Trust your belonging.

Visualize a flower opening on top of your head. See and feel rays of light entering your mind and body from the sun, moon and stars above. Feel how you are part of this immense, infinite Universe. Our bodies are made of the embers of burned-out stars that were released into the galaxy billions of years ago mixed with atoms from cosmic rays hitting the earth's atmosphere. We are literally made of stardust. Take a little time to allow that to fully sink in. Trust your belonging.

Now, bring your attention to your heart, perhaps caressing it gently with your hand or lightly tapping there to awaken this ever-so-important energy center. Recall the people, places, animals, beings, and memories that help your heart to open. Just allow whatever comes, all that which sparks the Love within you to ignite. Perhaps it is your child or pet, a deceased loved one, a spiritual figure…allow their eternal presence within your heart to align you with the energy of Love. Regardless of whether they are alive or deceased, in this dimension or another, nearby or far away, stop now and feel your everlasting connection, how they live within your heart. The love you shared is eternal, regardless of the circumstances. Trust your belonging.

Finally, open up now to the miracle of this Great Mystery that you are! Expand your awareness to perceive Great Spirit in whatever form resonates most with you: God, Buddha, Kali, Krishna, Jesus, Divine Mother. Allow your guides to help you remember your Divinity and to truly, deeply and fully trust your belonging.

Stay here as long as you'd like, just enjoying the feeling of your connection.

When you are ready, you can begin to come back slowly, feeling your body sitting on the chair or the ground, paying attention to your breath. Take your time, bringing back with you this sense of connection and belonging.

This practice is also available as an audio guided meditation to listen to, and is included with this book. Be sure to scan the QR code below to enjoy the audio meditation.

AUDIO: BELONGING meditation >>>>

YOUR BREAKTHROUGH PLAN FOR STEP 2

1. Do the Taking Stock Practice and listen to the Belonging Meditation every day.

2. Consciously use the tools you already have and take at least one step toward developing the new ones.

3. Commit to three actions you can take in the next week to reach out to the people you already have in your life and/or to find and develop a new tribe.

4. Once you've taken the initial steps, keep repeating them regularly while you focus on truly feeling your capability and strength growing, as well as your connection and belonging.

STEP 3:

AWAKENED HEART - DEVELOP EMOTIONAL INTELLIGENCE

"Your feeling of heartbreak is not neurotic, it is intelligent. It has something to show you that the unbroken could never reveal."

~ Matt Licata ~

STEP 3:
AWAKENED HEART – DEVELOP EMOTIONAL INTELLIGENCE

For me, this step is crucial and the area where I am most passionate. I often think of how different my own life and our world would be had we learned how to understand, regulate, and deal with our emotions as children. I would go so far as to say 90% of the problems and crises we face personally as well as collectively come from our severe lack of emotional intelligence. This isn't some statistic I am citing from an official source, but rather my own personal observation, experience and feeling. From depression, interpersonal conflict and addiction to poverty, destruction of the environment and war, our emotional ignorance is the root of so much of our suffering. It is one of the main causes of our disconnection from ourselves, the planet and each other.

Our emotions are the driving force behind our choices, relationships, and lives. They are what allow us to feel what it is to be alive and to be human. They are universal regardless of race, nationality, religion, gender, political affiliation, culture, financial factors, marital status, or any other division of our humanity. Everyone feels happiness, sadness, anger, fear, pain, joy, etc. This is true whether you are a wealthy businesswoman from Japan, a social and political activist trans person from Spain, or a good ole boy Republican from Texas. It doesn't matter on which ray of the very wide spectrum of possible ways to express and experience our humanity you find yourself. If you are a human being, then you have emotions; you feel.

Some feel more deeply while others have found ways to keep "the visitors" from showing up on their doorstep, at least temporarily, or at least we think we have. Most of us, either consciously or unconsciously, expend a great deal of energy trying to repress, avoid, ignore, and basically just keep as far away as possible those guests who aren't the "life of the party." We don't tend to do what Rumi suggests in his poem, "invite them all in laughing" and we certainly don't understand the idea that "they have all been sent as guides from beyond." Rumi and many other masters and teachers like him knew secrets that any of us facing difficulties would do well to learn: emotions are the key to unlocking our true potential…the gateway to resilience, depth, and wisdom, to our very core.

There are many apt metaphors for our emotions. Rumi calls them "the visitors." One very practical and helpful approach is to view them as aspects of our Inner Child, that part of us which was formed from our earliest childhood experiences.

The term "Inner Child" as it is used today in therapeutic and personal growth work was originally coined by the eminent psychiatrist Carl Jung in his extensive work, *The Archetypes and the Collective Unconscious* (Jung, 1959).

It is quite fascinating to observe in adults how, regardless of biological age, many of our thoughts, feelings and actions are still generated from this childhood perspective. It is most apparent in the conflicts we have with others. If you really observe a couple arguing or a power struggle at the office, you will discover uncanny similarities to disputes between seven-year-old siblings or children on a playground.

This is because many of us did not receive the kind of sensitive, empathic nurturing and support, unconditional loving presence, and emotionally intelligent guidance and encouragement that we needed as children. We probably didn't get it at home or at school. In fact, in many cases, we experienced the exact opposite. Even if we had our basic physical needs met, such as food, shelter and "education," our innermost needs were not. We weren't supported emotionally. This is not because our parents didn't love us or because there was something wrong with us as many came to believe, but simply because the adults in our lives were often emotionally ignorant as well. We received little to no guidance in interpreting our emotions, and the kind we did get usually taught us how to repress and avoid what we were feeling.

For this reason, our Inner Child is most often deeply wounded, filled with doubt and fear. In some cases, s/he is severely traumatized and acting out in destructive ways in your life. S/he is often at the center of the conflicts you have with others as well as your addictive habits. When we are going through tough times, this is the part of us that freaks out, over-reacts, or collapses into depression. It is continually and rather desperately re-enacting the patterns of abandonment, overwhelm, defense and manipulation that it learned in order to survive.

In the personal story that I described earlier about my jealousy breakthrough, I mentioned some of the inner parts I had encountered, including my inner child. What I came to realize was that a fundamental component of my suffering and struggle wasn't as much due to the parts that were playing out their stories, but more to the ones that were missing. My Inner Parent(s), the one who could protect, guide and care for the others, was virtually non-existent. I often enacted that role more with others than with myself, trying to play Mommy to my partners and loved ones. This often happens when we have developed the strategy of self-avoidance. We become "saviors" and mis-direct the energies of nurturing and care into this distorted version that tries to please, fix and (s)mother the people around us.

Or we just withdraw into our little bubble where we try to stay safe from being hurt more. We are terrified of our vulnerability, of our inner child's feelings, and we develop a plethora of ways to protect ourselves from feeling the

> *The wound is the place where the light enters you.*

pain. Whether it be food, sex, drugs, alcohol, work, Internet, or TV…our coping strategies and addictive patterns are our attempt to not feel the pain of our inner child. It is actually a rather creative and intelligent response, and it can work, up to a certain extent, for a limited time. The problem is, since these "solutions" are found outside of ourselves, they will never truly address the root of the problem, which is inside. We will find ourselves needing more and more ways of escaping the pain and dealing with the negative consequences that inevitably accompany them.

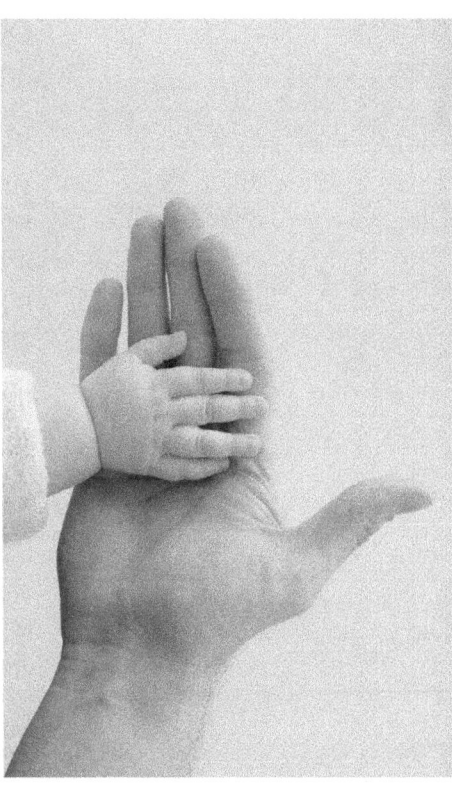

The only thing that will ever truly help us is to bring our own unconditional love and presence to that pain, to our fear, to the rage, our shame… to our inner child. We must become our own parent. We must act from the adult that we are and consistently, consciously, and carefully bring love and healing to the child within. I use words like MUST here even though they are words I usually steer away from because I want to stress how crucial this is. This isn't an exercise that we do once or twice and think we've done the work. As it goes when you are raising your own child, it is something that you do every single day, throughout the entire day.

EMOTIONAL NINJA TRAINING

The main feeling that most inner children share is a deep, gaping wound of abandonment, which is what most of us felt when our primary caregivers didn't show up for us consistently the way we needed. In psychology, this is referred to as the attachment wound (Karen, 1998). We tend to repeat what we learned and abandon ourselves over and over again. It is so habitual that it's almost like our default mode and our primary way of dealing with our emotions.

Whenever we feel triggered by something or someone, our internal dialogue usually goes something like this: "Oh, it's no big deal, just get on with it already" OR "That guy is such an idiot, just ignore what he said, it doesn't really matter" OR "How dare she treat me that way, I'm going to show her" OR "I am such an (idiot, bitch, cry-baby, fuck up, pathetic, insert insult here)" OR "Why bother trying, it doesn't make a difference anyway," and other such self-deprecating remarks.

These are the things we were told as children from adults who may have had good intentions, yet who actually taught us to minimize and avoid what we feel rather than learning from it, about it, about ourselves, about others, about life. These are subtle yet impactful ways we were abandoned as children and continue to abandon ourselves as adults.

Our coping strategies, our busy lives, as well as much of our inner dialogue are geared toward escaping from the uncomfortable things we feel. The faster and further away we run from the small, scared little one within, the more desperately alone, frightened and abandoned s/he feels. Even when you have succeeded in drowning her out, deep down you know she's in there, and she probably pops up when you least expect and in the most uncomfortable and inconvenient ways. Or maybe you've succeeded to such an extent that you no longer feel much of anything and, as a result, your life feels empty, hollow, almost pointless.

If you are going to turn your breakdowns into breakthroughs, you will have to connect and commit to your Inner Child. With all the patience you can muster and all the love in your heart, you can re-parent your Inner Child. We can end the agonizing cycle of abandonment now and form an unbreakable bond between our Inner Parent and Child that will bring us more confidence, creativity and calm than anything we have tried before. Only then can we respond from the mature adult that we are instead of collapsing into the small, helpless child from long ago.

Mindfulness teaches that our emotions are like waves in the ocean, rising and falling continuously while our Being or Consciousness is that of the Ocean itself. If we struggle and fight against the waves, we most likely will drown. We can learn to surf and ride the waves instead of being pulled down by them. As we do, the whole Ocean opens up to us and we realize how inseparable we are.

Now you're going to use my "Emotional Ninja Training" practices to cultivate your Emotional Intelligence.

Sometimes, especially when there is trauma and you are just starting to do this kind of deep, emotional work, it is recommended to be accompanied by a therapist.

Practice 1: R.A.I.N.

This is a Mindfulness practice that I learned from my favorite teacher on the subject, Tara Brach. Combining Western psychology and Eastern practices, she is the author of numerous books, such as *Radical Compassion: Learning to Love Yourself and the World with the Practice of RAIN* (Brach, 2020). I highly recommend her work. For me, it has been like a life jacket that prevented me from drowning many times throughout the past 10+years. I wish I had been taught these methods as a child. I sincerely hope that in the future we teach these practices to our little ones as they begin to experience the vast, unknown, and often frightening waves of their emotions.

This practice, in particular, has been one of the staples in my own process of emotional education. It is simple, profound, and effective and will get you well on your way to becoming an emotional ninja!

R – Recognize

Realize that some emotional button has been triggered. Maybe we don't know exactly what is wrong, but are conscious that something is unsettled within. Instead of just barreling on ahead (as most of us are conditioned to do), we pause and begin to shine the light of awareness within.

A – Accept and Allow

This is the crucial point where we do something different and commit to making space for what is coming up, even and especially when we don't like it. We say YES to ourselves, to the Life surging within us and to whatever is occurring. We stop running, stop fighting, stop all the ways we distract ourselves trying to hide from our Inner Life. Maybe it is uncomfortable at first, but we are no longer willing to abandon ourselves. We open our arms as we would to a little child who has come running to us crying out for help and we hold her in our gentle embrace. Whatever she is feeling is allowed, without judgment or punishment. There is a great sense of relief as we connect with love and safety.

I – Investigate with Kindness and Curiosity

We close our eyes and drop down into our body, out of our spinning thoughts. We scan and feel where the emotion is living in our body and focus on the physical sensations that accompany it.

We pay attention with curiosity to whatever information is wanting to come through. Perhaps we perceive a memory, an insight, a need.

We observe the train of thoughts rumbling around our mind. We ask ourselves, "what am I believing now about myself, the other person, life?" We question with intentional kindness, "is that really true?"

N – Nurture

We invoke our wise, loving inner sage and/or a spiritual being, friend or loved one who helps us to connect with safety, love, and a sense of belonging. We imagine that being or person holding us, or with their hand on our shoulder, caressing our cheek or in whatever way brings us a sense of peace and comfort. We can place our hand on our heart and feel the support, love and nurturing presence that comes through.

Practice Tip: This practice is best done as a kind of guided meditation in a quiet place with your eyes closed, but can also be done internally in the midst of a difficult situation.

My guided meditation of RAIN is available as an audio to listen to, and is included with this book. If you haven't already downloaded the audio, you can download it by scanning the QR code below.

AUDIO: RAIN guided meditation >>>>

On the following page is the transcript of my guided meditation version of RAIN.

Guided Meditation of RAIN

Closing your eyes and connecting with your breath. Allowing your body and mind to relax. Using your senses to arrive into your body and the present moment. Listening to the sounds around you, noticing the way the light filters through your eyelids, feeling your body sitting or lying down.

Now bring to mind a challenging situation that you recently faced. Choose something that was difficult, but not too major or traumatic, to practice with.

R - See the place, the people involved, what you were wearing, what time of day it was, all the details you can remember. Recall what happened that upset or triggered some difficult emotion(s) in you. What were you feeling...anger, fear, worry, grief, shame? Recognizing that we have been triggered is the first vital step.

A - Just recognize the trigger and allow yourself to feel it as fully as possible. Invite the "visitors" of your emotions to be there, allowing them safe passage. Accept what you are feeling, giving it permission to be just as it is without trying to fix, change or push it away. Imagine you are opening your arms and holding with love this small, upset part of you.

I - Feel in your physical body how and where these emotions live. Perhaps you notice that there are strong sensations in certain parts of your body. What can you feel…heat, cold, tingling, pulsating, pain, tension? Focus your attention there and feel the changing sensations.

Observe the thoughts running through your mind. When we are upset, they are often racing, repetitive and sometimes obsessive. This shouldn't be like this. That person did this and that means…Take a step back and observe the thoughts as though they were words on a page. Investigate with curiosity and kindness. What are the beliefs that generate these thoughts? What am I believing about myself, others, life? Begin to question them. Is it really true? Can I be sure that it's true? Have I felt this way before? When, with who? If this feeling had an age, what age would it be?

N – Continuing to focus on the breath, relaxing the body with each exhale and on each inhale connecting deeper within. Imagine that each inhale connects you to your Essence, your innermost nature and with each exhale you surrender into a field of protection and love that allows you to fully let go. Invoke or imagine your Higher Self and/or a loved one, ancestor, spiritual figure or an animal or pet that brings you a sense of safety and trust. Feel your bond and rest in the presence of their care. See yourself and the situation through their eyes and feel their support. Listen to any messages, guidance or insight that comes with an open and receptive heart. Bring that love and kindness to the small, triggered part of you.

Rest here in this field of belonging and connection as you visualize a light rain softly clearing the air and cleansing the space you are in.

Practice 2: focusing

Focusing is a technique that was developed by psychotherapist Eugine Gendlen (Gendlen, 1978) and allows us to use our body to process our emotions and connect with valuable insights to our difficulties.

It is best to sit or lie down, have your eyes closed or slightly open and start by connecting with the breath and relaxing the body. You can either start by thinking about a specific problem or situation that is troubling you OR you can allow your body to lead, first feeling the sensations and then allowing whatever guidance to come through spontaneously. Don't go into the mental story, stay with the sensations.

Turn your attention to the physical sensations moving around your body, scan through the different parts and just pay attention to sensations such as tingling, numbness, throbbing, pulsating, heat, cold, prickling, or whatever you can feel. Really direct all your attention to those sensations and then allow the one that feels most intense to be your main focus. Go deeper into that place in your body, where you feel the most...whether it's your hand, arm, chest, or back. Just stay there, breathing deeply and relaxing. Spend a few minutes feeling the changing intensity and sensations there. Really feel how it is in the body. Don't *think* about how it feels, instead, actually *feel* it.

What is the quality of the felt sense? If it had a color, what color would it be? If it had shape or form? What texture is it? Does it remind you of anything? Allow words, phrases or images to come through.

Stay in your body and just be open to whatever comes while noticing any release, insight, or change.

When you finish, you will find that you are calmer and perhaps have even had some important realizations about the situation.

Practice 3: Re-Parent Your Inner child

Find a comfortable position for your body. Inhale and exhale slowly, deeply, and consciously as you allow any tension in your body and mind to dissipate. Take a few moments here just breathing, relaxing, and connecting with the present moment. Allow any thoughts to just float away like clouds in the vast sky of your awareness.

Now recall an image or picture of yourself as a child. Allow whatever image appears and most calls your attention. Maybe you are very small, 3 or 4, or perhaps a little older. Pay attention to how they are dressed, the shoes they are wearing, how their hair is. Especially pay attention to the expression on their face and their body language. Are they standing, sitting, lying down, running, playing, hiding perhaps? Where are they, indoors or out? If they are in a room, what is the room like, what else is there? If they are outside, what environment is it, a garden, field, beach?

Now begin to perceive their emotions. How do they feel? Encourage them to show, tell, share with you whatever they are feeling. Tell them that whatever they feel is OK and that you are there to listen, to help. Be careful not to go into giving advice or telling them what they need to do or feel. Instead, focus on creating a safe space for them to express themselves fully, without restrictions. Encourage them to cry if they feel like it, scream or shout, to do whatever they feel they need. Ask them what they need from you and listen closely, without judgment to what comes out.

Validate their feelings and needs with your body language, your eyes, tone of voice, physical contact, and heartfelt intention. Let them feel you there, just listening, just transmitting love. Don't try to fix them, just be there for them. With your heart open, breathe deeply and allow your inner child to let out whatever it needs to. Invite them to come closer, maybe they want to sit on your lap, be held in your arms, hugged, or just to hold their tiny little hand.

Breathe with them, let them really feel your presence, your unconditional love, and your protection. Remind them that they are safe, that you are there, and you aren't going to let anything bad happen to them. Tell them how much you love them and how wonderful they are. Acknowledge their struggles along with their strength and innocence. Assure them that they are absolutely perfect just the way they are, a miracle of Life, a little shining star in the Universe. Tell them how happy you are that they are here, how valuable, and important they are.

Transmit all the love you can access to your Inner Child and allow them to soak it all up, as a little baby flower soaks up the rays of the sun.

Finally, when they are calm and feel safe, pick them up, holding them up above you. If they like it, you can even swing them around gently. Look deeply into their little eyes and feel your connection. Finally, slowly, carefully bring them down into you, merging their little body with yours and feeling your union.

Connect again with your breath, feeling your feet on the ground, body sitting or lying on whatever surface. Slowly begin to come back, taking your time, no hurry. When you are ready, open your eyes and gently stretch your body, bringing back with you a sense of wholeness and tenderness.

This practice is also available as an audio guided meditation to listen to, and is included with this book. If you haven't already, you can download it by clicking this link:

AUDIO: INNER CHILD meditation >>>>

"Please, Take My Hand"

Come closer my child, let me see you.
For so long you have been cast aside,
hidden away from the light of day
Living alone in darkness.
No wonder you're so afraid.
I can feel your trembling.
Sometimes it literally shakes me to my bones.
Come here, please, take my hand...
Shall we walk, together now toward the light?
One step at a time...
No hurry, no rush
It takes time to build trust.
I hear your cries
I want to listen
Remember how we stood together
in the center of the hurricane?
Even then, as the World
blew up around us,
we found that safe spot.
That is the power of our Unity.

~ Melissa Myers, 2016 ~

YOUR BREAKTHROUGH PLAN FOR STEP 3

1. Do each of these guided practices this week at least once, if not one each day.

2. Close your eyes and think of a color and two numbers between 1 and 21. Do this before you continue reading, please. Find or buy something that color that brings a sense of safe, cuddly, warm tenderness. The first number will represent minutes and the second number days. For x minutes during the next x days, hold that object and connect with your Inner Child, listening to, feeling and asking them what they need from you.

3. Throughout the days whenever you feel emotionally triggered or notice an emotion welling up inside of you, pause, place your hand on your heart and just breathe with it, offering love to whatever is coming up.

STEP 4:

SOUL ANCHOR - SPIRITUAL CONNECTION

*"When we open to love,
we become love."*

- Tara Brach -

STEP 4:
SOUL ANCHOR – SPIRITUAL CONNECTION

I have just come from the little shop near my house where I had a heartbreaking conversation with the owner, Sandra (name changed for privacy), who is currently undergoing the greatest crisis of her young life. Her husband was killed a few months ago in a car accident. He was 35 years old and leaves behind, not only her, but their two small children. They have been together since they were teens and have shared more than most of us can even imagine.

She explained how her own grieving had to be put on the back burner in order to plow ahead, keep her shop going and be the strong one to deal with the devastating reality that both she and her young boys were struggling to make sense of. She told me that she was not religious or spiritual and therefore found it especially difficult to respond to their heart-wrenching questions like, "Mommy, if God is so great, then why did he take my Dad?, "Does this mean I'll never have a father again?" She struggled to find some decent responses, while her own harrowing internal discourse was pleading to comprehend. "What did we do to deserve this? We are good, hard-working people, why us?" I held back my own tears as I listened to her, wishing there was something more I could say or do.

Her husband was Arabic, his family practicing Muslims, and she told me she had observed how they seemed to, through their faith, be able to access a little more peace amidst their pain and grief. But she didn't have that to hold onto. She was relying solely on her internal strength and the support of loved ones, trying not to completely shut down, despite what seemed like such a senseless, unfair, cruel event.

Perhaps there are other ways to come through the tragedies we experience, the crises we face and the incredibly challenging experience of being human but, honestly, I don't know them. For me, trusting that there is something Greater, beyond the small me, has been the fundamental pillar that has kept my world from crumbling in the face of adversity, change, loss, and pain.

Just saying that we are spiritual or going to church and practicing a specific religion is not the same as truly connecting to and trusting the Great Mystery. I like this Native American term, as it seems to most aptly express the spiritual realm that we each understand in our own way. Developing this connection and then choosing to trust it is a process. The path is unique for each of us, although I imagine that all paths eventually lead to the same place.

Oftentimes, it is the hardships and adversities of our lives that push us to discover and develop that spirituality. We can allow ourselves to break open so that, as Rumi puts it, "the light can enter."

I had a dream a couple of months ago that had such an impact on me that I haven't been able to stop thinking about it. In fact, I intentionally recall it as often as possible to help me continue learning to really trust, something that has not come easily to me. When you have been through trauma, we typically develop the opposite of trust. Our default mode is more one of alert, hypervigilance, control and all the protective mechanisms that we have found that provide some illusion of safety. Often under a well-constructed image of "togetherness" hides a terrified inner child who continually feels in danger.

In my dream, I was high up on the ledge of a steep cliff. A few of my friends were there telling me that we had to climb down. I was petrified and sure that I would fall. I racked my brain to think of another way but soon realized there wasn't one. The only way was to climb over a tricky overhang and then get your foot onto the ladder below it. Just as I feared, as I stepped over the ledge, I fell. As I started falling, I immediately felt myself being caught and held by several invisible beings. They carried me ever so gently down to the ground, set me down carefully, placing my hand behind my head. I opened my eyes slowly to find all my friends standing in a circle around me.

In the dream, I felt, as I have countless times throughout my life, that I was protected, that I was being guided gently and lovingly down to safe ground.

Of course, I have also felt quite the opposite. Something that has caused me great suffering is the same feeling that the woman from the shop and her little boys expressed…why is this happening to me, what did I do wrong and if God is so great, where is (s)he now when I need him and why is she doing this! I have come to realize that this mentality, this way of viewing circumstances, turns me into a victim, and God or the Great Mystery and Life itself into a tyrant who is somehow punishing me. The more I look at it that way, the more it becomes my reality.

I can remember what felt like endless nights through my early teen years lying in bed crying, desperately pleading with God to help me, and feeling that I was all alone. I formed a couple of very strong, debilitating beliefs during that time: (1) that I had been abandoned by everyone I loved, worst of all by God; and (2) that there must be something wrong with me.

These beliefs have tormented my existence and are at the root of almost every problem or conflict (internal and external) that I have had throughout my life. I know many others who have a similar story, an old, painful one that our inner narrator tells us over and over like a broken record.

As I grow, evolve, and mature into the wise, powerful woman I am becoming, I choose to see in a way that serves my life. I can then perceive all the ways that I have been loved and all the moments Great Spirit has guided me at forks in the road, protected me in moments of real or perceived danger, and helped me through the hard times. We can learn to tell ourselves a new story, one more fitting, more fulfilling, one that captures more of the true essence of who we are and what we are here for. We can see Spirit nowhere or we can see it everywhere. My prayer for a long time now has been, "Help me to feel You, experience You and trust You within me, everyone and life itself."

Many have come before us sharing their findings and leading the way. Profound insight, inspiration and encouragement can be found in countless texts and teachings on the subject. From traditional religions, esoteric philosophies, alternative new age ideas, Native American spirituality, or pagan, nature-based practices, there are endless fountains of wisdom and spiritual options to explore. In my opinion, the most reliable resource is our own personal experience. Once we open to Spirit, we begin to encounter it everywhere, in everything and everyone. We can do this through prayer, meditation, singing, dancing, writing and many other ways.

One of my favorite and most inspiring forms of experiencing God is through synchronicities. Carl Jung coined this term to describe, "the acausal connection of two or more psychic and physical phenomena." The following explanation comes from the website *www.carl-jung.net*:

> "This concept was inspired to him by a patient's case that was in a situation of impasse in her treatment. Her exaggerated rationalism (*animus inflation*) was holding her back from assimilating unconscious materials.
>
> One night, the patient dreamt of a golden scarab - *cetonia aurata*. The next day, during the psychotherapy session, a real insect hit against Jung's cabinet window. Jung caught it and discovered surprisingly that it was a golden scarab; a very rare presence for that climate.
>
> One generally speaks about coincidence in cases like this.
>
> But this coincidence is not senseless, a simple one. By using the amplification method, Jung searches for materials in connection with the scarab and comes to the concept of *death and rebirth* from the esoteric philosophy of antiquity.
>
> Thus the scarab is seen as a symbol of *deaths and rebirth* process that, in a symbolic way, the patient should experience for the realization of the completeness of her unilateral personality, the

cause of the neurosis she was suffering from." (www.carl-jung.net, n.d.)

I have many examples of this from my own life. I'll share a couple of them with you here.

When I was in my early twenties, I went through one of the first major waves of change and loss of my life. It included the death of both of my fathers and seven- year relationship with my partner, as well as the projects and dreams that mattered most to me. As a result, I was guided to leave the U.S. on a journey that would shake my very being to its core and in bumpy, messy jolts and stumbles, begin to awaken my inner wise woman.

First came the death of my stepfather, who had been just as much of a father to me as my biological one. I remember talking to my biological Dad on the phone afterwards and making him promise that he would be around for many more years as he was the only father I had left now. However, he was diagnosed with cancer just a couple of years later. A very aggressive brain tumor took his life after a long, painful battle. I went to Florida where he lived a couple of times in order to take care of him after the surgeries that attempted to remove the tumor which just kept growing back. This one had claimed his eye and, with his black patch, he looked even more like the pirate I had always suspected lived inside of him.

It was an incredibly difficult time for both of us. I was so young and really had no idea how to handle what was happening. He was fighting to hold on to the little bit of independence he had left while we both watched helplessly as his life slipped away. The best moments were those when the bald eagle came to visit us. I had never seen one in real life before. They make this very distinctive sound that cannot be mistaken. Whenever we would hear the call, we would come out of his trailer and go outside to watch them soar above us, coming quite close as if giving us a show. Just down the road from his house, she had her enormous nest high up in a big Southern Florida Slash Pine tree. We loved watching those eagles together. It was as though they somehow gave us strength and hope.

The day after I left from that trip to Florida, my father died. A few months later, I quit the band that had been my heartfelt dream up to that point and left the seven-year relationship with my boyfriend. It felt like my heart was breaking into a million pieces and the ground was crumbling beneath my feet. I started down a new path working with a wonderful woman on an exciting project that quickly grew near and dear to my heart but soon that was forced to an end as well. I began to feel restless and unsatisfied in every area of my life as disconcerting questions poured through my mind and troubled my heart. The kind of questions that Sandra from the little shop and her boys are currently asking. The kind whose answers are beyond rational explanation.

The last "shove" in that series of hardships literally propelled me off a cliff and, just as in my dream, I was caught and carried safely to the ground. On my way to a remote camping area in northern Arizona, my truck went off a very high precipice and rolled over several times down the steep embankment, finally coming to rest on a big, sturdy tree. The guy I was dating at the time was driving and my 10-year- old nephew was in the passenger seat. The truck landed upside-down, on its roof. We had to kick in the already shattered window to get out. We climbed back up the steep embankment, finally reaching the top just as the sun was setting. Miraculously, we were unharmed. I had some pain in my shoulder, but otherwise we all walked away literally without as much as a scratch. The vehicle was totaled. When the tow truck drivers came the next day, they looked at us in disbelief proclaiming that they could not believe anyone in that vehicle had survived.

Upon arriving back up to the dirt road, leaving the truck far down the mountainside below us, we realized that we were many miles away from the highway as well as our destination. It was getting dark, and we were shaken. I asked my boyfriend and nephew if we could form a circle, hold hands, and pray. Normally they might have chuckled at me or rolled their eyes, but after what we had just been through, they readily agreed. I earnestly thanked God that we were still alive, that we had survived and then requested more help. Night was rapidly descending, it was getting dark fast, and we were in the middle of nowhere, too far from anywhere to walk. As soon as we finished, we saw headlights in the distance coming closer. An old pickup truck pulled up with two young guys in it. The three of us stared in amazement at the vehicle covered with large bright painted words, Jesus lives, Long Live Jesus, God is Glorious and a plethora of these kinds of Christian phrases. Astonished, we turned to each other and in a low incredulous voice I murmured, "Wow, ok, well, thank you, Jesus."

For months before the accident, I had been perceiving these kinds of signs and synchronicities urging me to travel. The first guy I dated after leaving my boyfriend was in a band called, "Traveler." He spent several months out of every year traveling to different countries and studying the music there. He told me stories of foreign lands and life experiences that began to awaken a curiosity and impulse within that I had never felt before.

The book, *The Alchemist* fell into my hands. This epic tale, written by Paulo Coehlo, tells the story of a young shepherd who embarks on a quest and "along the way, learns to listen to his heart and, more importantly, realizes that his dreams, or his Personal Legend, are not just his but part of the Soul of the Universe" (Arroyo, 2008).

I met three friends at a concert who had spent the last five years of their lives traveling around the world. My best friend and I joked that they reminded us of Jesus, Buddha and Krishna. Each of their stories inspired me to spread my own wings and explore new horizons.

I started to feel an urge, an inner calling, a longing. An unshakeable feeling began to grow within that maybe this was something I was meant to do.

The accident, being that close to death, was the final catalyst that really made me question where I was headed, with who, and why. What was the purpose of all of this, of my life? Was I really happy? Who was I and what was I here for?

I wasn't sure, but I felt in my heart and soul that I needed to try to find out. All that had defined who I was up until that point -- which had given me the relative sense of safety that most of us hide behind for protection -- had started to crumble.

I recently saw in a video where a man explained that the only reason the lobster grows is because his shell becomes too small for him and increasingly confining and uncomfortable. He finds himself under pressure, more and more uncomfortable and therefore has to cast off the shell again and again in order to continue being able to grow. The narrator remarked that if the lobster had doctors, then it would just go and get a Valium every time it was uncomfortable, and so it would never grow. Our very discomfort is oftentimes the indicator of an opportunity calling for growth.

> *The mother eagle teaches her little ones to fly by making their nest so uncomfortable that they are forced to leave it and commit themselves to the unknown world of air outside.*
>
> - Hannah Whitehall Smith

I was scared though, unsure. Where would I go? What about my life in Arizona? I had just met a man I really liked, what about him? What about my friends, family, my Mom, brother, my nieces and nephews? I was very close to my people; they were everything to me.

And so, I went up north to a little town called Cottonwood, to a place called Sycamore Canyon for a hike. At the top of the hill, before descending, I called out to Spirit to guide me once again, to show me clearly if it was my "destiny" to go on this journey. I requested a very specific sign that I couldn't misinterpret. I asked to see a bald eagle. I had been living in Arizona for almost ten years at that time, spent tons of time in nature and had never seen one. About 45 minutes into my hike, I stopped by a little stream to eat my lunch and I immediately heard her distinctive call. There, perched on a tree stump, just on the other side of the creek, was a big, beautiful, bald eagle staring right back at me.

Needless to say, I took that journey and many years later, here I am writing about it.

Perhaps these kinds of things have happened in your own life, albeit less obvious, but you just chalked them up as coincidence. But what if there really is more to it?

When you are going through hard times, connecting to Spirit can be a true lifesaver. And if you've never been a very spiritual person and are going through a crisis, maybe it is a good time to allow something bigger than your little self to shine through the cracks shattering your world. Our inner child needs our inner parent. And our inner parent needs to know and trust her connection to the Universe, to something bigger, beyond her fragile human existence.

Einstein said, "There are two ways to live your life. One is as though nothing is a miracle. The other is as though everything is a miracle." When we are connected to Source/God/The Universe/Spirit/The Great Mystery or whatever you want to call it, we get what Einstein is saying on a very deep level and it completely changes our lives.

My life experiences have shown me that there's far more to existence than the mundane routines or harsh realities many of us feel trapped by. We are more than we often realize, and Life itself holds incredible depth waiting to be discovered -- if we take the time to explore. Spirituality reveals an entirely new dimension to both our struggles and our lives. In turn, our struggles deepen and enrich our understanding of Spirituality.

My dear friend Mali has often talked to me about Carlos Castaneda, author of *The Teachings of Don Juan*. One of those teachings refers to the assemblage point (Castaneda, 1968). As I have been researching the topic, I realize it is quite deep and complex and with so little knowledge I cannot attempt to explain it well. However, I bring it up because the way I understood it when she explained it to me has been very helpful in my own times of crisis.

It alludes to the position from which we view and respond to ourselves and the world. We can interact with life from the small, scared, separate self or from the perspective of our soul, the eternal part of us directly linked to God. How we interpret and experience what happens changes drastically depending on the point of view from which we situate ourselves.

When I am going through hardships and find myself struggling and suffering, I remember this and ask myself, "from which point am I positioned now seeing/experiencing what is happening?" I then visualize almost like an energetic pole within me that I can consciously choose to recalibrate to align with my Soul.

From there, I listen to my intuition, which we could say is the language of the soul. I allow it to speak to me and guide me, almost like a wise inner teacher who knows secrets beyond what my logical mind can perceive. When I am aligned with my Soul, listening to my intuition, life seems to make more sense than when I am trapped in the worries and conditioning of my mind. I feel more calm, confident, and clear and there is a kind of flow and magic to the moments.

> *The intuitive mind is a sacred gift, and the rational mind is a faithful servant. We have created a society that honors the servant and has forgotten the gift.*
>
> - Einstein

SEEING THE SIGNS SYSTEM

Most of us have experienced or said to another, "I just have a hunch or a feeling that I should…" That is the voice of our intuition. Try following it and see where it leads. Usually, it directs us to precisely the place we need to go. It also speaks to us through our dreams, longings, and even physical sensations. At first it may come as a faint whisper, but with practice you will fine tune your ability to listen to and follow the voice of your soul.

The following practices make up what I call my "Seeing the Signs System." They are specially designed to help you tune in to the messages and guidance of Intuition and the Wisdom of The Universe.

Practice 1: Guided Meditation
Opening to Spirit and Handing Over Our Crisis

Go out into nature. It could be a forest, beach, park, or garden. Any place where you can see, smell, and feel nature will do just fine. Find a comfortable place to sit or lie down and connect with your breathing. Feel the breath coming in and going out while connecting with your body and the ground beneath you. Allow Mother Earth to cradle you as you open your field of awareness. Listen to the sounds around you fading in and out; birds singing, breeze rustling through the trees and the steady murmur of your own breath. Absorb the warm rays of sunlight and feel the breeze gently caressing your skin.

Gently close your eyes and begin to imagine the Spirit of the trees, flowers, and stones around you transmitting love, wisdom, and support. Open to feel your connection to everything around you, to feel how you are part of it all and all of it is a part of you. Choose one part of Mother Nature to link your full attention to. It could be a stream, a leaf, a tree, flower, stone, branch or whatever you would like. Just open to whatever comes, noticing what you feel and receiving any guidance or insight that may arise.

Turn over your current problem or crisis to this Greater Intelligence and ask for help. You can literally imagine that you are handing it over to God and that she is taking the heavy burden from you so that you can lighten your load. Trust that your guides are there, listening and supporting you during this difficult time.

When your mind becomes distracted, just bring it back, lovingly, and persistently. Re-focus on your breath, the sounds, and the present moment, again and again as we continue training the thinking mind to open to Spirit and serve our Soul.

Practice 2: Perceiving Intuition

Tuning in to our intuition means forging a kind of bond with ourselves that we are often not used to. Most people nowadays are continuously plugged in to all kinds of technology, interacting through the Internet with people all over the world. While this can be wonderful, unfortunately, for many, the channel to their Inner World is completely forgotten. If we want to harness the power of our Intuition and see the signs that guide us on our way, we will need to come back home to ourselves and open to the life happening around us.

Our intuition is our inner compass that guides us in the right direction. It is beyond our rational mind and is connected more directly to our Soul or Essence. As with most aspects of our Soul, it is more subtle, coming through almost like a whisper.

It can be helpful to determine how you receive and perceive this guidance. To do this, you can explore the four claires: Clairvoyance (seeing), Clairaudience (hearing), Clairsentience (feeling), Claircognizance (knowing).

Very simply put, some people are especially visual and will be drawn to something or someone because it catches their eye. For others, sound is the key. This could be hearing something within telling them to go right instead of left or to call their friend who just at that moment was thinking about them. Some of us are feelers and we can meet a person and sense when to open up and when to keep our distance. And the last are those who just know. It's as though a kind of sixth sense or gut feeling urges them to take that risk or play it safe.

In the coming week, pay close attention to your senses and open to which ones seem to catch your awareness more than others. Try following guidance that you receive in this way and see what happens.

When you have a decision to make, of course you can make your list of pros and cons and think rationally about it as usual while also opening to your Inner Guide.

Try placing a couple of pieces of paper face down on the ground with the different options written on the down side. Mix around the papers so that you don't know what they say. Stand up, close your eyes and take a few deep breaths connecting to your Inner Guide. Open your eyes and look at the papers on the floor, see if anything about the way one looks calls to you. Listen to see if you can hear some kind of whispers coming through from your Soul or if you just know which paper you need to pick up. Stand on top of each one and just feel what you feel. Perhaps one brings a feeling of peace, while another brings anxiety or pain.

Finally, take a look at the paper that called to you and consider that as a message from your Intuition or Inner Guide.

This is a way you can see which of the Claires is your main guidance system. Perhaps it's a mix of several or all of them, but usually one is predominant. Keep playing in this way to get to know and begin to discover your Soul's own inner language.

Practice 3: Seeing the Signs (Synchronicity)

For me, synchronicity is like the signposts along the way that let me know I'm headed in the right direction. For the next 40 days, you are going to open your awareness and pay close attention to the way your Soul, Source and Life itself are guiding you.

I gave you the example of the eagle on my hike in Cottonwood, Arizona. Here is another simpler example from my own life. In 2013, I went through another deeply transitional and excruciatingly difficult moment in my life, perhaps one of those bigger crisis moments where I was struggling with intense fear and anxiety on a constant basis and was diagnosed with CPTSD (Complex Post Traumatic Stress Disorder).

I took a trip back to Arizona to visit my family. In the bedroom I was staying in, there was an old alarm clock radio on the bedside table. One day I was in the room crying and just feeling the deep despair at how lost I felt. I said out loud, it's like I'm just on the wrong frequency or something, totally out of tune.

In that exact moment, the radio started making this loud chirping static sound as if it were trying to find the signal! I laughed out loud and was able to connect with some hope that even though I felt so disconnected, I was reaching out and trying to be reached back. I was not alone.

Think back now throughout your own life and see if you can remember any of these kinds of little signs. Don't worry if you can't remember any. Sometimes we're so busy, we often miss them. If you can remember any, write them in your journal. Either way, begin to ask regularly for your Soul Team to show you signs and pay close attention so that you don't miss them.

Practice 4: Soul Pole Alignment

Oftentimes we find ourselves pulled around by our varying inner voices. The wounded inner child and inner critic are ones that habitually run our lives without us even realizing it. We've already talked about working with the Wounded Inner Child. The best way is to hold space for him/her infusing them with as much love as we can muster.

The Inner Critic often needs the same attention, as it too is usually a young, wounded version of ourselves developed to protect us. This voice for many has become so habitual that we barely realize it's not our true voice. Its pervasive and debilitating remarks can destroy our self-esteem if we allow it to go unchecked.

One simple, yet effective way to work with it is to begin to pay attention to the criticism going on in our minds, about ourselves and others. Then, we can say to ourselves or out loud, "My Inner Critic doesn't like my hair today" or "My inner critic says I'm too fat, skinny, young, old, whatever" or "My inner critic says my significant other should be like this or shouldn't do that." (Inner critics love words like should, have to, shouldn't, must -- so be on the lookout for those. They can be an alarm reminding us that our Inner Critic has taken the mic).

When we acknowledge it is the Inner Critic speaking, we separate that part of us from our True Identity. Just as in working with the Inner Child, now is the time for the conscious adult to take the reins.

Finally, we can align with our soul. I called this exercise the Soul Pole Alignment because we can literally visualize it like a beam of light, energy, color, or a pole that aligns us from Earth to Sky and beyond into the Universe. We can picture a literal shift in our awareness from that of our smaller selves to that of our Infinite selves aligned with Source. We can adjust our "assemblage point" as Castaneda described it so that our perception is no longer taken hostage by our wounded inner child but, instead, are able to view things from the higher perspective of our Soul.

Just close your eyes and visualize a beam of light coming from the Sun/Moon and Stars, whatever color you choose. Imagine that you are transported out of the Earth's atmosphere along that beam of light, all the way out into the vast, immense, infinite Universe. There you are united with your Essence, your Soul, the part of you that feels how it is beyond time and space, how it forms part of everything that ever was, is and will be.

> *Wisdom tells me I'm nothing, love tells me I'm everything. Between the two my life flows.*
>
> - Nisagardata

YOUR BREAKTHROUGH PLAN FOR STEP 4

1. Do each of the practices at least once, if not one each day.
2. Create an altar or shrine in your home. It can be simple or elaborate. You can have pictures, images or objects that help you feel more connected to Spirit, in whatever way works for you, perhaps with incense, candles, crystals or stones. You could include a picture of yourself as a child.
3. Each day spend time in front of your altar meditating, praying, journaling or reflecting.
4. Ask Great Spirit to show you signs and keep your senses open to perceiving them.

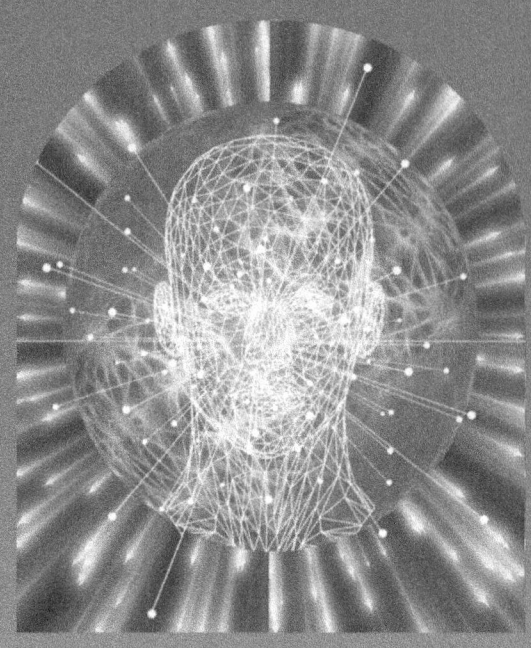

STEP 5:

MIND OVER MATTER - ATTITUDE

"We are what we think. All that we are arises with our thoughts. With our thoughts, we make the world"

- Buddha -

STEP 5:
MIND OVER MATTER - ATTITUDE

We may not be able to choose what happens to us in life, but we can choose how we respond to it. This takes a great amount of practice and de-conditioning as so much of the time we are unconsciously reacting to the circumstances of our lives. We have the power to choose our attitude and we must learn to do so if we want to harness the lessons from the storm.

Part of our ability to survive in this world comes from our reptilian brain and limbic system, which are wired to continually be on the lookout for what's wrong or what could go wrong and try to protect us. Beyond mere survival, we have the capacity to thrive, to grow, to create, to rise and shine. Neuro-scientifically speaking, we would say that this comes from the prefrontal cortex, the newer, more evolved part of our brain where compassion lives. We can learn to use our mind effectively. Instead of allowing our survival instinct's fight or flight mechanism to become a trap that chains us in stress, anxiety, and conflict, we can consciously activate the more evolved part of the brain and move into new territory - beyond survival into thriving.

We have awareness and therefore the ability to rewire, recalibrate and choose how we view ourselves, each other, our circumstances, God, and the world. Our minds are powerful and it's up to us to train them accordingly, to question our thoughts and beliefs and to choose our worldview and attitude carefully.

We are part of an immense Universe, more of it unexplored and unknown than the miniscule speck that we inhabit and know as planet Earth. We form part of this Great Mystery and yet much of our own inner world, our minds, emotions, and behaviors are just as enigmatic as outer space.

We strive for certainty, control, and logical explanations for something as wild, mysterious, and awesome as life itself, yet we rarely undergo the inner exploration that allows us to experience it for ourselves. This Great Mystery cannot be caged and placed neatly into a tidy little binary box where good and bad, right and wrong and black and white are clearly defined.

People are capable of the most beautiful, inspiring, incredible feats, as well as the most heinous, despicable, and hurtful acts. This world we live in is made up of all of it and so are we as human beings. We have co-created all of this from our ignorance, greed, fear, and selfishness, as well as our love, generosity, fortitude, and courage.

It is easy to fall into victimhood or to become angry, bitter, and hardened by the tragedies and trials of this world. Life is not easy. No one ever said it was supposed to be. There is both immense beauty and wonder, as well as immeasurable suffering and injustice. I don't know why it is that way. Perhaps some of the great masters who have come before us have left some clues. It is said that light cannot exist without darkness and vice versa.

Regardless of the reasons why, the reality is that it is that way. We can resist and reject it, or we can embrace and learn to live with it. In addition, we can take it a step further and consciously participate in making it the best it can be, in making ourselves the best we can be. What we bring to this life and what we get out of it is, in large part, up to us and depends on our attitude and what we put into it.

We have so much more power than we realize. How are we going to use it?

> "We but mirror the world. All the tendencies present in the outer world are to be found in the world of our body. If we could change ourselves, the tendencies in the world would also change. As a man changes his own nature, so does the attitude of the world change towards him. This is the divine mystery supreme. A wonderful thing it is and the source of our happiness. We need not wait to see what others do."
>
> ~ Mahatma Gandhi ~

Yesterday, I bathed in the Cantabrian Sea, finally letting go of some of the heaviness I had been carrying, allowing the water to hold me up, just floating gently beneath the wide-open blue sky. I remembered the Mindfulness teachings about how our True Essence is the Ocean. The waves come and go, rise and fall. Sometimes big ones seem to threaten to pull us under and it can be frightening. But from the perspective of our Ocean-like Essence, we know that we have the capacity to be with the waves. They are a part of us, the temporary, ever-changing element of our being, while our true nature is the immense Ocean itself.

That bath in the sea was a total attitude adjustment for me. I had been struggling for the past week with some very difficult situations that had occurred in my local community. As a result, I had unconsciously adopted a negative, hopeless, desperate mindset that was pulling me down into a very dark place. My dear friend, Marina, defined this as "humanophobia" -- that profound sadness, disgust and rejection of the world and humanity. It felt like a deep disappointment, in myself and fellow humans.

I felt like my little world had suddenly turned upside down. It was as though the beloved place where I lived full of wonderful people who I considered my family, had been replaced by a chaotic, hostile, twisted version filled with selfish assholes, violent perpetrators, and angry hypocrites. In our attempt to "right the wrongs" occurring in our little patch of society, we had instead started to turn against one another, perpetuating the very violence we were protesting against.

It felt terrifying and enraging for my inner child who had experienced some of those things growing up and tried so desperately all her life to control from happening again. But, as Einstein said, "No problem can be solved from the same level of consciousness that created it." The level of consciousness of the inner child cannot solve our problems, as it is the source of the very attitude that created many of them. Our wounded inner child lives trapped in her fear, pain, rage, and separation, in her suffering. Her reptilian brain is the one who runs the show, anxiously trying to keep her safe in what she perceives as a dangerous environment. It isn't her fault and it's up to us to help her find her way back to safety.

In those violent situations that had occurred in my village, it was other human beings, just like myself and my friends, who were reacting from their pain, from their wounded inner child. Perhaps it is a mirror for the unattended violence we are all carrying within, albeit secretly. If we hope to resolve these situations, we must attend first to our own wounded inner child and then position ourselves in the adults that we are: responsible adults who embody the attitude of humility, willingness, empathy, courage, and respect. Adults who know how to place and honor healthy boundaries, communicate effectively, and respond instead of react. Adults who make conscious choices and take conscious actions.

We all form part of this world, whether we condemn it or defend it, love it, or hate it, actively participate in it, or hide ourselves away. We are responsible for each grain of sand we bring to and take out of the big playground of life. No one is to blame, and yet we all are. We cannot pretend to bring peace to our world, to end poverty and war until we first face it within ourselves.

> "It may be important to great thinkers to examine the world, to explain and despise it. But I think it is only important to love the world, not to despise it, not for us to hate each other, but to be able to regard the world and ourselves and all beings with love, admiration and respect."
>
> ~ Hermann Hesse, *Siddhartha* ~

As conscious adults, we must be willing to go through whatever comes our way, to face the inevitable pain, to feel it and allow it to break us open.

Embedded within the most profound darkness shines an infinity of stars. We are part of both that darkness and that light, made up of the same stuff as the Universe itself. Oftentimes, it is the pain and our willingness to be with it, that reveals this to us. The greater truths do not come to us on the surface, but in the depths of darkness.

Maybe we don't always get to choose what happens around us or to us, but we do get to choose what we do with it. We get to choose the attitude we adopt to face the challenges along the way. We get to choose if we respond from our Soul awareness, from our Oceanness, or if we become completely identified with the waves, fighting futilely against them, and eventually drowning beneath them. We decide if we allow our wounded inner child to run our lives, or if we step up into the adult capable of acknowledging, holding, protecting, and re-parenting her/him. We get to decide if we become the victims or the victors.

There is a Native American parable called "The Two Wolves," attributed to the Cherokee tribe:

> An old man is teaching his grandson about life. "A fight is going on inside me," he said to the boy. "It is a terrible fight, and it is between two wolves. One is evil – he is anger, envy, sorrow, regret, greed, arrogance, self-pity, guilt, resentment, inferiority, lies, false pride, superiority, and ego."
>
> He continued, "The other is good – he is joy, peace, love, hope, serenity, humility, kindness, benevolence, empathy, generosity, truth, compassion, and faith. The same fight is going on inside you – and inside every other person, too."
>
> The grandson thought about it for a minute and then asked his grandfather, "Which wolf will win?"
>
> The old Cherokee simply replied, "The one you feed."

> *Feel it, don't feed it.*

I wouldn't necessarily call this good and evil as the parable does, nor do I think that some emotions are bad and others good, that some should be pushed away. I think of them more as visitors, as Rumi describes, or as Inner Children. However, it does aptly illustrate the power of our choice and the attitude we choose to nurture. If we want to break through the crisis in our lives, to rise up no matter how many times we break down, it is crucial to cultivate an empowering attitude. To feed our soul instead of our ego. To take responsibility for our inner world instead of getting stuck in blaming the outer one. To choose when to stand up and set boundaries and when to step back, zoom out and gain perspective.

It has been many years now since I embarked on my own inner journey. I have struggled through long corridors of what, at times, felt like an infinite underworld. My mind has been jumbled with flashes from the past projected into the future. Deep-seated emotional issues which had developed in early childhood turned into phobias that made going to the store or having a meal with people feel like a dangerous mission. My attitude became bleak, and I started to believe I would never find my way out. The more I believed that, the more I locked myself into a cell. I was feeding the wrong wolves, and they were consuming me.

I learned that neither feeding them nor running away from them helped. I am learning now to train those wolves and therefore access their true power.

When it comes to our emotions, I have found that the most effective attitude is to *feel it but don't feed it!*. Attend to the inner child, go into the body, and feel what is asking for attention, stop and be with the feelings but do not feed the stories.

The stories of who is right or wrong, of why things are the way they are, of why this is just more proof that you will never be OK. You know the stories, the ones that loop through our racing minds and pull us into a dark pit of suffering. Feeling pain is part of being human, resisting it or getting caught in it, exaggerates the pain and feeds suffering.

When it comes to our thoughts, we can learn to slow them down, observe and guide them to a place we consciously choose. As with a wild dog or horse, when you first start, it will pull and run off in one direction or another. But with time, persistence, and dedication, they will follow your lead.

Mindfulness teaches that we don't have to believe our thoughts. They are often not true, but rather conditioned programming from the past, looping over and over like a broken record.

According to psychologist Shauna Shapiro, we have 12,000 to 50,000 thoughts per day, 95% of which were the same as yesterday! (Shapiro & Carlson, 2009).

We are reliving our past repeatedly instead of experiencing the only time we ever really, have which is NOW. We are condemning ourselves to a future based on our past instead of creating one based on our soul's purpose or heart's true desire.

Over the course of the past year, I have been experiencing a profound personal transformation, what could be called a Phoenix Process. We go through many of them throughout our lives. Times when everything that felt like steady ground seems to crumble and who we were no longer fits who we are becoming. It is uncomfortable, to say the least. Sometimes, it is excruciating. To meet the current circumstances, we have to expand, grow and sometimes break through decades, maybe even lifetimes of conditioning, habits and patterns. The symbol of the mythic Phoenix captures well the alchemy of transcending crisis. We must shed our old skin and rise up from our own scorched ashes into in a new, more powerful version of ourselves.

> *It is always darkest before dawn.*

They say, "It's always darkest before the dawn" and that has certainly been my experience. Before we can be reborn, we have to go through death. It is not easy to let go of the old…whether that be people, situations, or parts of ourselves. Yet this is an inevitable law of life. All that is born will die. Perhaps it is the only thing we know for certain. When we have forged and nurtured our spiritual connection, we begin to trust that just as outer space is infinite, so are the limitless possibilities of what is beyond death. Somewhere deep within, we know that death is also just a new beginning, and we can relax into a kind of trust that diminishes our fear.

At the beginning of 2022, I reached one of those moments in my life. My business was flailing, as well as my friendship with my business partner as we scrambled to avoid it drowning under the weight of Covid restrictions. Money was scarce. My nervous system had reached well past its limit after the previous year of leaving my partner of six years and my home, moving several times, and beginning a new relationship. My mental health was failing as my CPTSD flared up with intensity at all these changes, grief, and uncertainty. There was an especially dark moment when I really just wanted to die. I made an important decision. I was not going to commit suicide so, therefore, the only other option was to continue living. I had to make some significant changes in my life, my way of doing things and especially my way of thinking. My life depended on it.

I signed up for a coaching program designed by an incredible woman named Marisa Ruiz, which has truly changed my life. At the end of the book, I will include a valuable list of the main lessons I learned through the program that have helped me tremendously and I'm sure will help you. Some of the teachings in this book are based on them. Also, upon her recommendation, I began studying the work of Dr. Joe Dispenza. I highly recommend his work to understand the power of the mind and the latest studies from neuroscience and neuroplasticity on how to create lasting changes in the brain with the way you think.

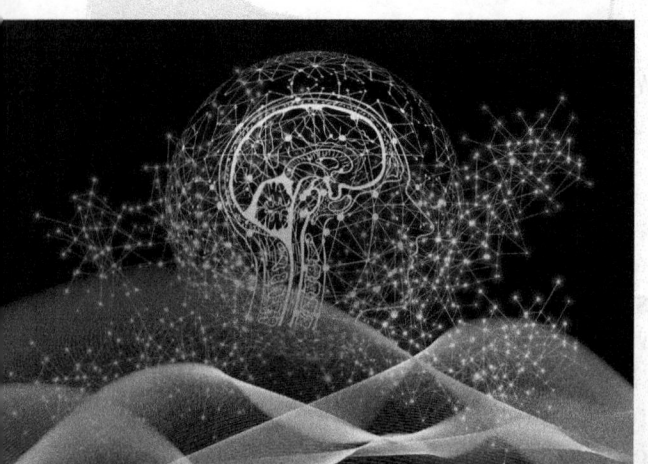

Some of the valuable lessons include truly understanding the importance of the phrase, "Where attention goes, energy flows." What we think and what we feel instigate what we do, converting into who we become, which in large part creates the life we are living. Dr. Joe calls this our "state of being" (Dispenza, 2012). If our thoughts, day after day, are mainly focused on our problems -- what we lack, what's not right about us, our loved ones, or our lives -- then our reality becomes a self-fulfilling prophecy based on negativity. If our thoughts are specifically aimed at gratitude, love and who we want to become, then everything changes for the better. Our feelings, actions, "state of being" begin to reflect that new, consciously-chosen reality and our lives dramatically improve. In his book, *Breaking the Habit of Being Yourself* (2012), Dr. Joe gives numerous examples of cases where patients have healed from illness, chronic anxiety, and a wide variety of debilitating conditions.

Personally, I have experienced profound changes in my own well-being and life since I have been applying these teachings. I learned about "positive thinking" over 20 years ago. To be honest, for many years I hadn't given it much credibility, chalking it up as some of the New Age airy fairy stuff that sounded good but didn't really work. In fact, I was concerned that it was another form of "spiritual bypassing" (using spiritual concepts to skip over necessary inner work). When experiencing grief and hardships, nobody wants to be told to just think positive, nor is it appropriate advice for many moments of our lives.

During my coaching program and through Dr. Joe Dispenza's work, I have acquired a new understanding of neuroscience and quantum physics that has made a dramatic difference in my life. One of the epiphanies for me was the realization that I had been living most of my life in an attitude of survival instead of truly living. I am finally reprogramming that tendency, learning to flourish and thrive. I hope this book will help you do the same.

The "Attitudes & Beliefs Transformation Package" has three practices that will help you shift from surviving to thriving.

Practice 1: Attitude Quiz

How can you tell if your attitude is helping you to breakthrough your current crisis or bringing you down and turning you into a victim?

Here's a little quiz to check:

1. Do you often find yourself ruminating about the past and projecting negatively in the future?
2. Do you compare yourself to others, feeling inferior in some way?
3. Do you complain often and blame others, society, or your past for your problems?
4. Do you feel and express gratitude regularly?
5. Do you feel like you have a black cloud over your head?
6. Do you blow things off as if it doesn't really matter, while deep down you feel upset about it?

7. Do you distract yourself compulsively with food, social media, Netflix or other addictive habits instead of dealing with the challenges at hand?

8. Do you tell yourself it's all someone's fault...yours, your boss, friend, parents, partner's, and so on?

9. Do you believe the negative thoughts that swim around your head and buy into your inner critic's view of your life?

If you answered yes to many of the questions above, it's time for an attitude adjustment.

You can start by doing the Attitude Adjustment Practice and then following the Breakthrough Action Plan at the end of Step 5.

Practice 2: Attitude adjustment

When I was a little girl, my Mom used to tell me I needed an attitude adjustment. That's when I knew I was really in trouble, hahaha. As an adult, I realize I regularly need to give myself one of these, in the most careful, loving way possible. Here is a practice to help you realign your attitude with your adult self and your Oceanness/Soul.

Gather together some paper and colored pencils, crayons or markers.

Close your eyes and connect with your Inner Child and his/her emotions regarding what is happening in your life. Using your non-dominant hand, allow whatever comes out on the paper to just be expressed, without holding back, trying to control, or critiquing it. Just let it come out. Give yourself at least ten minutes.

Now, close your eyes again and come back to your adult self, the age you are now. Use the Soul Pole technique we learned earlier and visualize a beam of light coming from the Sun/Moon and Stars, whatever color you choose. Imagine that you are transported out of the earth's atmosphere along that beam of light all the way out into the vast, immense, infinite Universe. There, you are united with your Essence, your Soul, the part of you that feels how it is beyond time and space, how it forms part of everything that ever was, is and will be. From that perspective, take a look at the situation you are currently facing. Using your dominant hand, allow yourself to express what you see, feel and realize from that view on the paper. Give yourself as much time as you need.

Finally, go back to the first drawing and ask your Inner Child what she needs and add it to the drawing. Go back to the second drawing and add something to represent your Inner Child, including him or her in the connection to your Soul.

Fold the two pictures together or hang them somewhere where you can see them regularly.

3 Practice 3: Uprooting Limiting Beliefs

A big part of what generates a negative attitude is the limiting beliefs that we unconsciously carry within us.

Some typical examples of beliefs we commonly have about ourselves are: "I'm not good enough"

"I should be more…" "I shouldn't be so…"

"I'm never going to be able to…" "I'm always…"

"I'm not very smart, artistic, fun…"

Examples of beliefs we commonly have about others:

"women are…"

"men are…"

"you can't trust people"

"he/she should/shouldn't be, do, say, etc."

And beliefs about life in general:

"Life is hard"

"bad things always happen to me"

"you've got to fight to get ahead"

These are just a few examples of the beliefs that generate our attitude and ultimately create a large part of our reality. What we believe, we perceive. If I believe I'm not good enough, I will feel that way, act that way and my life will reflect that back to me. If I believe people can't be trusted, that is what I will experience.

Most of the time, we aren't aware of the beliefs that are running our lives. So, the first step is to uncover them. How? Well, how we are feeling is a good place to start. When we are feeling exaggerated emotions of any kind, that is usually an indicator that there are some unconscious limiting beliefs operating behind the scenes. Using the RAIN practice, we can tap in and begin to reveal them.

Once we have brought them to light, the next step is to question them. Byron Katie has books and programs dedicated completely to this process which she calls *The Work*. The main thing is to ask yourself, "Is it really true? Can I be 100% sure that this is really true or is it something I was told as a kid and just adopted unconsciously? Is this something I still want to believe, or has it outlived its shelf life? Is this belief serving me or is it holding me back?"

We can then choose to let them go. I literally picture myself turning them over to God or my Higher Self or Mother Earth…into the river, or fire or blowing them away in the air.

For this process to work, it has to be done over and over again. Some of these beliefs have been lurking in our subconscious mind since we were toddlers. If we want to reprogram them, we will have to consistently reveal them, question them and let them go. We can choose our new beliefs, the ones that are more adequately aligned with who we are now and who we are becoming, the ones that serve and empower us.

YOUR BREAKTHROUGH PLAN FOR STEP 5

1. Do each of the above practices at least once, if not one each day.

2. Regularly count your blessings and practice gratitude. Start and end each day by taking a few minutes to do this. Don't be mechanical about it. Really feel it.

3. Be very mindful of your thoughts. Whenever you catch yourself in negative self-talk, stop and bring your mind back as you would a dog on a leash, lovingly, firmly, back to the place you consciously choose to focus. Keep your mind more on the present than the past.

4. Question the beliefs those thoughts reveal, ask yourself, "Is this really true?" Perhaps it reveals the old programming that we are working to release. If so, let it go. Remind yourself that it isn't true, just something you believed once upon a time that has caused you enough suffering. Let it go. You can visualize yourself blowing it out like dark smoke or throwing it into a fire or river.

STEP 6:

TRAINING & PRACTICE

*"Knowing is not enough; we must apply.
Willing is not enough we must do."*

~ Goethe ~

STEP 6: TRAINING & PRACTICE

There is a big difference between talking about being positive, reparenting our wounded inner child, being present, and improving our lives versus truly making the embodied choice repeatedly in each moment to put it into practice.

Things we have been learning throughout this book (such as kindness, compassion, opening to what is coming up, and holding it with love), may or may not be novel ideas. However, for many of us, truly practicing them is, indeed, very new.

For this to help, we must actively practice believing in and encouraging our progress. We do this by taking steady baby steps, marking, and celebrating each small degree of change. We become our own cheerleader, our own best friend, and our own leader. Therefore, we commit to ourselves, to our process and have the perseverance and determination to not give up, no matter how hard it seems or how long it takes.

Difficult times are when we most need to put into practice the things we have learned up until now. That means integrating it, doing it, applying it on a regular basis, training ourselves and consistently committing to our process. I stress this point because I realize how many things I learned conceptually yet did not actually put into practice. It was as though I thought just by "getting it" mentally, something would magically change in my life. It doesn't work that way. You have to use it, you have to do it. We are building new muscles, and this is done through repetition, patience and dedication.

Just a couple of months into the trip that took me out of my "comfort zone" and into the intense inner and outer journey that I've been on for over 15 years since I left the U.S., I met a beautiful man in the Sahara Desert in Morocco. We spent a night together under the immense sky full of stars which seemed to illuminate our minds and hearts. I had a boyfriend at the time, so our encounter was a purely philosophical one, albeit with a deep, intimate, heartfelt tone rarely found in even the closest relationships. We shared our hopes, dreams, fears, insights and ideas about love, life, and our futures.

We closed the evening with a simple yet wise plan for going forward. "Say It, Believe It, Do It, Inshallah." Inshallah is an Arabic word that can best be translated as "God Willing."

We know that "what we practice grows stronger." As with the story of The Two Wolves, if we are practicing anger, fear, jealousy, and so on, they will grow stronger. If we are practicing love, joy, gratitude and so, on, they will also grow stronger. Practicing love means not judging, condemning, and criticizing our habits and patterns or our wounded inner child's emotions such as anger, fear and jealousy. It means becoming aware of our patterns and reprogramming them.

It means paying attention, holding space for and re-parenting our wounded inner child. This takes a deep, determined commitment and lots of training. Our conditioning and the habits we have developed is to do the opposite. It's up to us to re-program ourselves.

When we are triggered by some difficult situation in our lives, our sense of security is threatened, and our limbic system takes over. The default setting can get stuck in reacting, such as freaking out, closing down, avoiding and repressing or some combination. If we want to learn to respond instead of reacting, to thrive instead of just survive, to break through instead of break down, we must access the more evolved parts of our brain and create new paths.

THE BREAKTHROUGH ROADMAP

The old path is familiar as we have walked it thousands, maybe millions of times over the years. It is well worn and it's the one we automatically head down whenever we want to go somewhere. Maybe it takes us to dark, difficult, and horrible places but, as they are familiar, we are drawn to them. Maybe it just keeps us going in circles, but we have gotten used to it. Or maybe it takes us to dead ends, but we know them well and so they feel safer.

The new path is unknown, unfamiliar, and uncertain. Our minds don't like that, they prefer certainty. As we talked about before, our reptilian brain, wired for survival, wants to keep us safe. For that part of our brain, safe is equivalent to familiar. If we want to thrive, to go beyond mere survival, to breakthrough our suffering into freedom, we need to do something different. We need to create new paths which requires commitment, perseverance, dedication, determination and consistency. It requires practice.

We head down the path on automatic pilot, taking us into the same old story. With Mindfulness, we wake up from our sleepwalking and consciously choose a new path, creating a new story.

Our thoughts, beliefs, actions, and patterns can be reprogrammed. In neuroscience, there is a well-established theory developed by the Canadian psychologist Donald Hebb, which states, "Neurons that fire together wire together." (Hebb, 1949) Hebb's research showed that as neurons in our brain are activated time after time, they form increasingly stronger connections. In this way, as we repeat the same experiences, thoughts, and feelings, our brain learns to strengthen and improve the neuron networks associated with those experiences. Dr. Joe Dispenza refers to this as going from thinking to doing to being. (Dispenza, 2012)

We can literally rewire our brains, reprogram our habits and create a new story, even in the most challenging of circumstances. The way to do that is to consistently use the new tools we have acquired, keep building the hero muscle and bringing awareness to our habitual default patterns. It doesn't matter how long we have been stuck in the old story or lost on the old path. It is never too late to begin again. Each day, each moment, each difficulty is our opportunity to redirect our thoughts.

Now you're going to use "The Breakthrough Roadmap" ...three powerful practices that I have put together to help you forge your new path and your new life!

Practice 1: Old Path New Path

Gather two pieces of paper and some colors. Take a few minutes to center yourself, using your breath as we have been doing together throughout the book. On the first piece of paper, draw the old path, the habitual one, the one you have been going down over and over again for years. Perhaps it's a dead end, a circular path or a narrow lane. Just allow whatever comes out without censoring. Include in the drawing the specific objects that form part of the path. They can be symbolic or literal like a TV, a scared bunny, bottles of beer, or a raging river. Again, just allow your subconscious mind to express itself without filter.

When you are finished, take a few deep breaths and integrate.

Then, connect with the new path you are creating. Consider some of the new habits you have been forming throughout the past few weeks or months. Think about where you are headed, where you want to go. What is your deepest intention for the journey you are on? Now, draw the new path. Allow whatever comes without holding back. Include specific objects or symbols to represent tools, mindsets and actions that help you stay on the new path. At the end of the path, draw something that represents your goal, such as the gold at the end of the rainbow.

Finally, you can draw the two paths in such a way that the new one really stands out and lights up (just as the new neural pathways in your brain are beginning to do) and the old one fades out. Perhaps plants are growing over it and it's barely noticeable because it's being used less and less.

My niece, Alina Wagner, described the process of changing our habits and the neural pathways in our brain like this:

> "The usual path (the one you want to change) is wide, open and well beaten from it being the automatic route. At the end of the road, it starts out as a strong connection to the bright yellow neuron. Once the person decides to change the normal route, they have to create it completely from scratch. It starts out as a little game trail, still overgrown with a bitty trail that is just exposing itself with a weak connection to the neuron at the end. After the forest greatly resisted the new trail in the beginning (trying to grow over and cover between trips), it finally begins to allow it. Over time, the bitty game rabbit trail becomes more and more worn, widens, and opens to where it's now the easier path with a strong connection to the neuron. As this happens to the new trail, the forest starts taking back the old path. It begins growing over it and closing in with weeds and tree branches. Then this trail finally smalls to just a little game trail with a weak connection. Eventually it just disappears completely, and you would have never known there was a path in the first place."

When you have finished, take a few deep, cleansing breaths and integrate the experience.

Hang both pictures in a place where you can see them to help you remember what supports you as you create your new path and what pulls you back onto the old one. The idea isn't to feel bad about and judge the old path. It's just to be aware and have the possibility to choose.

Practice 2: Commitment

Find a nice piece of paper, either one you draw or find online and print. Write your commitment to yourself for the process you are currently undergoing. Sign, date it and hang it somewhere you can see it regularly.

Example: I, Melissa Myers, commit to my daily practice of the three daily check-ins, exercise at least four times per week, regular yoga and somatic practices, as well as monitoring my thoughts to keep me aligned with the present moment and who I truly am.

Practice 3: Plan

Write out your plan for putting into practice the new skills, abilities and habits that support you on your journey. Be as detailed as possible. You can write a daily, weekly and monthly plan which includes activities to add to your schedule, negative patterns to be on the lookout for and ways to counteract them. Include what you have learned so far that supports you to harness the opportunities from your current crisis.

YOUR BREAKTHROUGH PLAN FOR STEP 6

1. Do each of the above practices at least once, if not one each day.

2. Pause and really observe your path, commitment and plan each day. Put your energy into it, feel it, believe it, do it, Inshallah!

3. Be diligent and committed, as well as flexible and forgiving with yourself. This is a process. Extremes are bound to cause failure. If you just blow it off, it won't work. If you take a military approach to it, it probably won't work either. Find your rhythm, your balance, and your flow. Be consistent and don't give up.

4. More than WHAT you do, be aware of HOW you are doing it. The more you train yourself to be present, the easier it will be to notice when you've fallen back into old programming, and you will be able to bring yourself back to the new that you are creating.

5. CELEBRATE EACH SMALL STEP AND CENTIMETER OF PROGRESS THAT YOU MAKE ALONG THE WAY!

STEP 7:

SERVICE - SHARE YOUR WISDOM

"How wonderful it is that nobody need wait a single moment before starting to improve the world"

~ Anne Frank ~

STEP 7:
SERVICE - SHARE YOUR WISDOM

As Anne Frank so courageously reminds us, no matter how challenging our own circumstances may be, we can always be of service to others. In fact, this is precisely one of the great gifts that we receive from the crises we overcome in our lives: the chance to share with others the wisdom and insights that we earned. It brings a great sense of meaning and purpose to our own lives and can make all the difference to other lives.

I have learned and continue to learn a great deal from my own personal experiences. This is how we manage to grow and mature. Yet, the insights and wisdom shared by those who have gone before is what has really kept me going when it seemed impossible. It has given me the impetus to push through some of the most difficult roadblocks along the way. The music, books, videos, audios, workshops, courses, paintings, poetry that have appeared on my path have provided me with the inspiration, motivation, and fundamental comprehensions needed for me to persevere.

> *We make a living by what we get, but we make a life by what we give.*
>
> - Winston Churchill

This is what a true hero/heroine does. She goes out, faces the dragons, darkness, and dangers, which require her to face all that is within and therefore become equipped to step up into the highest expression of herself. Then and only then can she do her part to "save the world." I don't mean that we are literally supposed to save anyone, but rather connect with our mission to give what only we can give.

This means taking what we have learned, gained, and developed and offering it back as part of our sacred duty to Life Itself.

We do this just because deep within us we know it is what we are here to do. Being of service feels good, it feels right, it feels deeply fulfilling in a way little else does. The world needs each of us to rise up from the ashes of our own ruins, shed our old forms and be reborn like the Phoenix to help shine the way forward for our fellow humans.

Martin Luther King, Jr., said it so well, in his speech of February 4, 1968:

> "Everybody can be great. Because anybody can serve. You don't have to have a college degree to serve. You don't have to make your subject and your verb agree to serve. You don't have to know the second theory of thermodynamics in physics to serve. You only need a heart full of grace. A soul generated by love."

In doing so, we fully integrate our own lessons, and we offer a beam of light that may just save another's life or at least help guide them through the darkness as others have done for us. This can be done in both simple and sophisticated ways.

Perhaps it is just the kind of compassionate, non-judgmental listening that we can offer to another because we are able to understand in a way that others who haven't been there cannot. Or perhaps the poem we posted on social media reached deep into the heart and sparked the soul of other human beings struggling to find their way. It could be as simple as a smile or as comprehensive as a book or course.

What matters is that we share our treasures, great or small. In sharing, they multiply for all.

Haha…that sounds like a Dr. Seuss rhyme!

I'll follow that up with an appropriate poem from the character and book with the same name, *The Lorax*:

> "Unless someone like you cares a whole awful lot, nothing is going to get better. It's not."
>
> ~ Dr. Seuss, *The Lorax* (1971) ~

SHARE YOUR GIFTS FORMULA

The final step involves stepping up and giving back. It means rising and shining. It is where we give the gift of ourselves to life and humanity.

To help you, I have created the "Share Your Gifts Formula" with these three important practices.

1 Practice 1: Preparing to Serve

Make a list of what you have gained, learned, and developed through the current crisis you are going through or past hardships. Then ask yourself how those qualities, insights and abilities can potentially serve others/The World.

Practice 2: Pay It Forward

Many years ago, around the year 2000, I saw a movie that deeply impacted me which became one of my all-time favorites called, *Pay it Forward*. If you haven't seen it, I highly recommend it. The plot revolves around a young boy from a troubled family who is inspired by an assignment given by his teacher to design a plan to make the world better. His idea is to do a selfless act of service for three people. Those three people have to do the same and pay it forward to three more people so that this kindness chain extends and grows.

Now it's your turn. Within the next three weeks, less than 21 days, your assignment is to pay it forward. Give back in whatever way you feel inspired to three different people.

Practice 3: Ikigai

Some years ago, a student introduced me to the concept of Ikigai, a Japanese term that roughly translates as "reason for being" or "reason to live."

Ikigai (pronounced "ICK-ee-guy") is, above all else, a lifestyle that strives to balance the spiritual with the practical.

This balance is found at the intersection where your passions and talents converge with the things that the world needs and is willing to pay for (for those developing their professional path). You could replace pay for with, willing to receive.

Check out the diagram and take some time to reflect and write about your own reason for being and how you can harness your particular set of skills, abilities, experiences, passions and motivations to give back to the world.

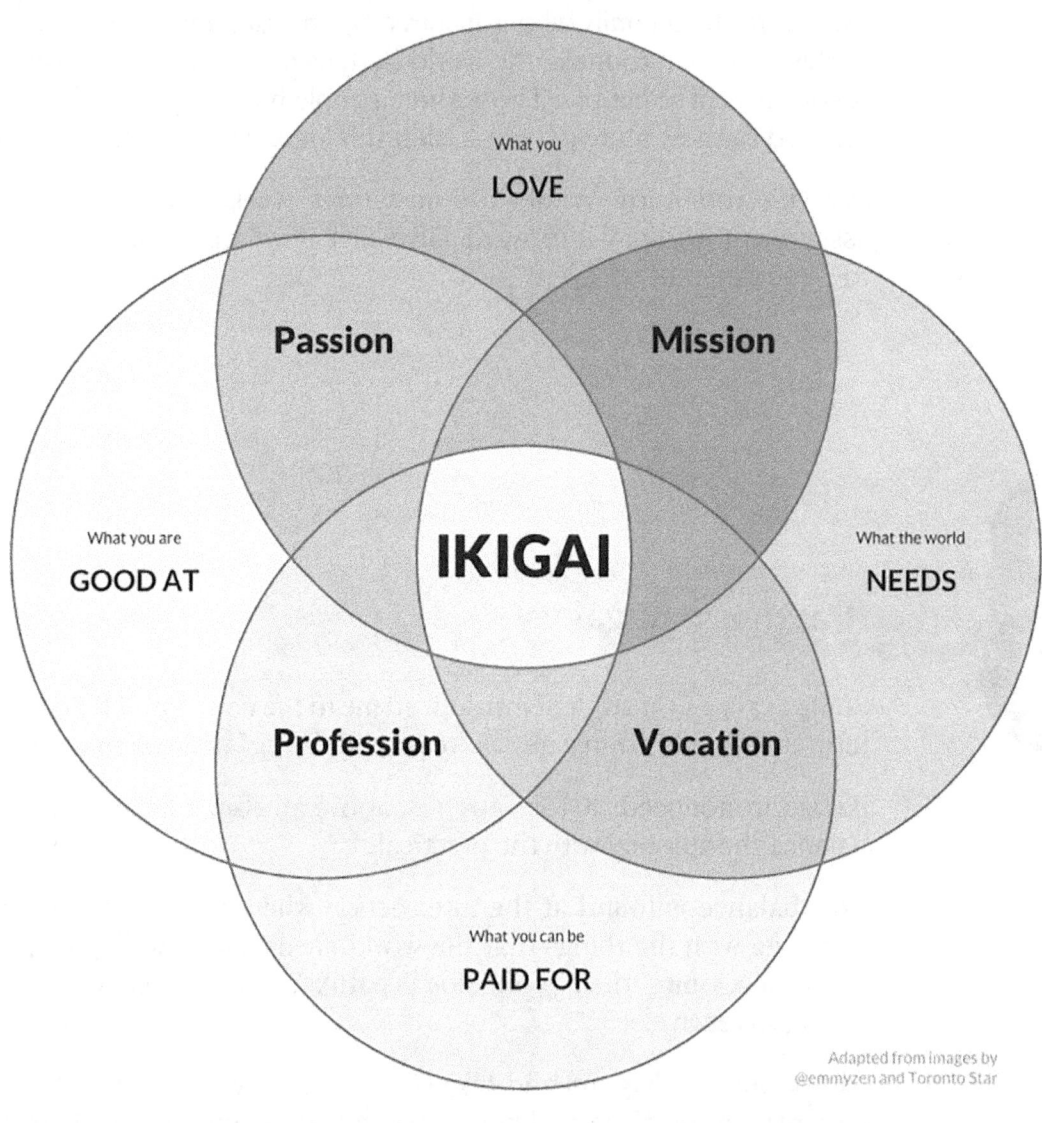

YOUR BREAKTHROUGH PLAN FOR STEP 7

1. Do each of the above practices at least once, if not one each day.
2. Reflect on your ability to give and receive in the different areas of your life: personal relationships, community, work, love, sex, and so on. Write about it in your journal.
3. If you have found this book useful, perhaps you could gift it to another person whom you feel it could help.

CONCLUSION

"Hardships often prepare ordinary people for an extraordinary destiny."

~ C. S. Lewis ~

CONCLUSION

Crisis often comes as a result of conflict, change, loss, and death, which are inevitable and necessary parts of life. They are not problems to be overcome, but fundamental life experiences on this planet. They are opportunities for growth, depth, and awakening. They can be our greatest teachers. There is absolutely no one who doesn't have to face these events sooner or later. The question is, how do we face them? As victims of circumstance, a brutal world or a cruel God? Rather, do we embrace them, learn from them, and grow into the version of humanity we long to encounter in the world?

Embracing them means we open our hearts wide enough to hold all of it. It means we allow what is to be, give space to our feelings, honor the process, and practice again and again the art of letting go, stepping back and rising up. It means we adopt an attitude that serves us and life, instead of one that keeps us down believing in the illusion of our separateness.

In this book, I have outlined seven practical, powerful steps to help you turn breakdowns into breakthroughs and learn to weather life's storms.

This isn't something we do once and for all and live happily ever after. It is something we have to do over and over again, each day, each moment. We have countless opportunities throughout our lives to practice. The more we do, the more natural these steps become.

> *Our greatest glory is not in never falling, but in rising every time we fall.*
>
> - Oliver Goldsmith

When I am using these steps or some variation of them, no matter what life throws my way, I am able to find my way through and come out on the other side more fully myself and more alive than ever before. When I don't use these steps and I fall into the old, conditioned path, then I feel lost, and I suffer tremendously.

My suffering is often the wake-up call that helps me realize that I have gotten off track and remember that I can choose to come back. As a survivor of childhood trauma with CPTSD and chronic anxiety, sometimes I have to do this many times a day. Every time I do it, I am being the heroine of my story.

As the novelist and poet, Oliver Goldsmith said in the 1760s, "Our greatest glory is not in never falling, but in rising every time we fall." (Quoteinvestigator, 2014)

No matter how many times we get off track, fall down and lose our way, we can always get back up and begin again. The darker it gets, the closer we are to dawn. When the cocoon becomes too small, we break through and spread our newly formed wings. When the old skin (or mask) has worn out, we shed it, revealing a deeper layer, closer to our true identity. When the flames burn us to ashes, we regenerate and rise again.

The storms of life are inevitable, but without them we couldn't learn the true skills of navigation and discover all the hidden treasures of this great adventure.

That is the hero/heroine's journey, our journey.

Reminders as you go forth on your way…

1. Change, the deep lasting kind, happens little by little in small, firm, consistent steps.

2. In order for those small steps to take root, the new path to become more familiar and habitual, CELEBRATE your progress, and encourage and support your Inner Child.

3. Impatience and the tendency to mistakenly view the old habits and patterns (as they inevitably come up) as proof that you can't change is a trap that keeps you stuck in the old story.

4. You can't wait to feel "safe" in order to take action and believe in your progress. Believe first in your capability, in the process and your progress in order to gain confidence. You are training yourself to believe in and trust yourself and life.

5. When you get triggered, pay attention to the habitual reaction, like rushing and falling back into old patterns. Instead, stop and attend to what's coming up. Sometimes, do exactly the opposite of what the habit is pushing you to do. For example, instead of going faster to avoid facing whatever is triggering you in the moment, stop, breathe, and feel.

6. Take your commitment seriously and choose your perspective carefully.

7. FEEL IT, DON'T FEED IT!

8. Ask for help when you need it. *Trust your belonging*.

9. Say it. Believe it. Do it. Inshallah.

10. Be immensely kind to yourself.

"Beyond the Edges"

Somewhere out past the lines and confines
imposed by our minds,
exists an infinite field of possibilities.
I have tasted this place
ever so briefly...
Fleeting glimpses into the heart of eternity.
Felt the river pour through me,
emptying and filling me up time and again,
carrying me out beyond the walls
of time and space.
I have touched my edges,
pulled back in fear
only to put my hand back into the flames,
looked down to see my burning heart
exploding with sadness, gratitude, fear, and love
breaking through,
melting the icy walls of separation.
And as I lean into it,
opening wider
let the rays of sun kiss the wound,
I feel how I really can just let go.
Standing still,
wrapped in the silence
that leaves space to listen,
I hear the beating of my heart
grow stronger, louder, faster
as I take another step toward the edge...
I remember why I'm here.
A wave of life surges through me
and I become the song
that rises up and out of my soul.
Loosening my grip
on the rails of false security,
Awe and wonder-filled,
arms raised,
I leap into the immensity —
into the abyss
of infinite possibilities.

~ Melissa Myers, 2013 ~

ABOUT THE AUTHOR

Melissa Myers is a certified Transpersonal Psychotherapist, Life Coach, Spiritual Counselor, Reverend, Reiki Master, Yoga and Mindfulness Instructor with a degree in Communications.

She has been working with clients through a private practice since 2012.

She is a published poet and author of *The Path Part 1: The Inner Journey*, and *Lessons from the Storm: 7 Steps to turn Breakdowns into Breakthroughs* and contributing author of Amazon #1 Best Seller, *Wisdom of the Silver Sisters*.

For the past 18 years, she has been living in a small village in Spain working as the Founding Director of Relax in English LLC, offering retreat style English Immersion Courses to Spanish business leaders based on Mindfulness and Emotional Intelligence.

She has more than 25 years of experience organizing and imparting retreats, workshops, and a variety of events.

Her own path led her through many experiences which contributed to awakening, from a very young age, with an intense interest in the human condition. For this reason, she has devoted her life to exploring psychology and spirituality. Her passion to understand herself, life, and humanity on a deeper level, as well as deep connection with nature, have been her greatest inspirations.

Melissa is a survivor of childhood trauma, including sexual abuse and domestic violence, and continues her own healing journey learning from and bringing love to the resulting CPTSD and Erythrophobia.

CONTACT MELISSA

If this book has helped or resonated with you, and you would like to explore the possibility of working with Melissa in Individual Private Sessions via her Breakthrough Coaching Program.
Feel free to send her a message at: melissa.myers77@hotmail.com
Or visit her website at: www.breakthrucrisis.com

BIBLIOGRAPHY

Arroyo, A. P., & Chazelle, D. ed (2008, December 28). *The Alchemist (Coelho) Summary*. Gradesaver. https://www.gradesaver.com/the-alchemist-coelho/study-guide/themes.

Brach, T. (2019). *Radical Compassion: Learning to Love Yourself and the World with the Practice of RAIN*. Viking Life (Penguin).

Castaneda, C. (1968). *The Teachings of Don Juan: A Yaqui Way of Knowledge*. University of California Press.

Dispenza, J. (2012). *Breaking the Habit of Being Yourself*. Hay House. Frankl, V. (2006). *Man's Search for Meaning*. Beacon Press.

Foster, T. C. (2003). *How to Read Literature like a Professor: a Lively and Entertaining Guide to Reading Between the Lines*. Harper Perennial.

Gendlin, E. T. (1978). *Focusing: How to Gain Direct Access to Your Body's Knowledge*. Everest House.

Gordon, J. S. (2019). *The Transformation: Discovering Wholeness and Healing After Trauma*. Harperone.

Hebb, D. O. (1949). *The Organization of Behavior: A Neuropsychological Theory*. John Wiley & Sons.

Jung, C. G. (1959). *The Archetypes and the Collective Unconscious. (The collected works of C.G. Jung, Volume 9, part 1)* Routledge & Kegan Paul.

Karen, R. (1998). *Becoming Attached: First Relationships and How They Shape Our Capacity to Love*. New York: Oxford University Press.

Kubler-Ross, E. (1969). *On Death and Dying*. New York: The Macmillan Company. Lesser, E. (2005). *Broken Open: How Difficult Times Can Help Us Grow*. Villard.

Levine, P. A. (n.d.). *What is Somatic Experiencing?* somatic.experiencing.es. Retrieved September 19, 2021, from https://somatic.experiencing.es/en/.

Maté, G. (2010). *In the Realm of Hungry Ghosts: Close Encounters with Addiction*. North Atlantic Books.

Quoteinvestigator. (2014, May 27.) *Our Greatest Glory Is Not in Never Falling, But in Rising Every Time We Fall*, https://quoteinvestigator.com/2014/05/27/rising/#note-8986-12.

Shapiro, S., & Carson, L. E. (2009). *The Art and Science of Mindfulness: Integrating Mindfulness Into Psychology and the Helping Professions*. American Psychological Association.

www.ingramcontent.com/pod-product-compliance
Lightning Source LLC
LaVergne TN
LVHW061343060426
835512LV00016B/2639